Living in the Presence and Principles of Christ

Discover Your Personal Significance through the Indwelling Power of God!

Dr. Susanna M. G. Bell, Ph.D.

© 2014 by Dr. Susanna M. G. Bell, Ph.D.

All rights reserved including the right of reproduction in whole or in part in any form or by any means without the prior written permission of the author, except by a reviewer who may quote brief passages in a review to be printed in a newspaper, journal or magazine.

Cataloguing-In-Publication Data:

Title ID: 4552946

ISBN: 1494352893

ISBN-13: 9781494352899

1. Significance 2. Image 3. Spirit & Soul 4. General

Printed by Create Space, an Amazon Company

Manufactured In

USA   Great Britain   Europe

To Place Individual or Bulk Orders,

Go to: https://www.createspace.com/4552946

Dedication

To my sons, Victor, Lamont, and Bryan for the exceptional commitment and fulfillment you bring to my life.

To my beloved granddaughters, Erinn, Elise, and Nyah, my precious gifts from God, who share their love, joy, and inspiration continually.

To other loving, compassionate family members and friends for your words of encouragement and motivation throughout this endeavor.

A special tribute to Dr. LeVonder P. Brinkley, a phenomenal author, for sharing her expert advice and enlightenment.

Table of Contents

Preface — ix

Introduction — xi

1 God Designed You for Greatness! — 1

2 Predestined for Victory: Spirit, Soul, and Body — 11

3 Abundantly Blessed by His Grace — 47

4 Renewing the Mind–A Lifestyle Experience — 75

5 Understanding Your Soul — 89

6 Reborn to Reign in Christ — 105

7 Living in Kingdom Faith — 127

8 Encountering the Supernatural — 151

9 The Anointing of the Holy Spirit — 173

10 Operating in Kingdom Prosperity — 185

About the Author	191
A Seven Day Intercessory Prayer Journal	193
References	211
Bible References	213

"For I know the thoughts that I think toward you, says the Lord, thoughts of peace and not of evil, to give you a future and a hope."

[Jeremiah 29:11]

Preface

As believers, we have a responsibility to set the example for Kingdom living here on earth. God created us in His image so that we could live in harmony with His plan for our life's journey. As you probably know, His first creation failed the obedience test. Are we going to make the same mistake? The world would not have an "identity crisis" if we returned to Christ, our redeemer. It is not enough to just exist in His presence; we have to live by his principles also if we desire to enjoy an abundant life.

The essential premise of this book is to enlighten and encourage believers and non-believers to have confidence in the truth that we are deeply loved, highly valued, and totally significant to God. When we recognize whose we are, then we will accept who we are as children of God. [1 John 4:17] says, *" Love has been perfected among us in this: as He is so are we in this world."*

My desire is to empower and compel the body of Christ to advance to the next realm of their Kingdom assignment. First, we have to receive the revelation that we are loved and highly favored before we can live effectively in the manifestation of His promises and principles. My hope is to saturate you with the love of the Lord so that the enemy will have no place. Our spirit was transformed when we were born again, but our soul (mind, will, and emotions) constantly need renewing to keep us from returning to the "old man" again.

These inspirational pages will increase your desire to have a Spirit-filled encounter with Jesus. You will have an unquenchable thirst to be made whole in every area of your life-spirit, soul, and body. Hopefully, you will live the highest level of life possible as you learn to truly appreciate living in His presence while being guided by His principles.

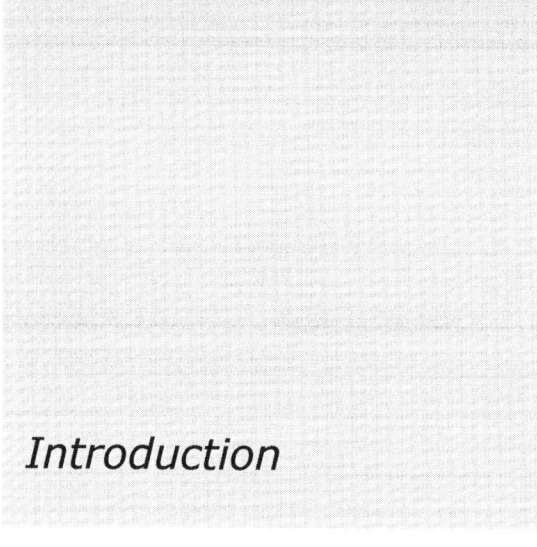

Introduction

LIVING IN THE PRESENCE AND PRINCIPLES OF CHRIST

Everyday we live in God's presence physically, with an amazing opportunity to be enlightened by His spiritual principles as well. The truth of the matter is that God wants you and me to triumph in the essence of who we are by realizing whose we are. When we learn who we are in Christ, we will no longer hold hands with mediocrity, nor will we bow down to impoverishment and insufficiency. *[Jeremiah 29:11] NKJV states, "For I know the thoughts that I think toward you, says the Lord, thoughts of peace and not of evil, to give you a future and a hope."*

God has a wonderful plan for your life! In order to receive it, an intimate relationship with Christ has to be established. Several principles, which are Biblical teachings or standards, have been established as evidence to let you know how valuable and significant you are to the Father. God loves us so much that He chose us in Him before the foundation of the world, that we should be holy and without blame before Him in love. [Ephesians 1:4]

Living in His presence is another way of saying that God has adopted us as His own children. He brought us into His own family and made us heirs along with Jesus. Through Jesus' sacrificial death on the cross and His resurrection, we received redemption and forgiveness by God's grace through faith. We didn't earn it nor do we deserve it. As heirs, we have value and significance; we are abundantly blessed and highly favored. God has raised us up together, and made us sit in heavenly places in Christ Jesus!

Living according to His principles or teachings is what believers do to show appreciation and reverence for what God has done for us. He adopted us because He is a good Father. As His children, we should be concerned with how we choose to live in His presence. God's principles were given to keep us safe, not to condemn us. Obedience to ethical and moral standards leads to a long, productive life. I contend that we should not just exist in His presence, but we should also thrive by living according to His godly standards and principles.

One

GOD DESIGNED YOU FOR GREATNESS!

Just like Adam and Eve, you were designed to live eternally. The first family was created to live in God's image and so are we. They lived with God's favor, protection, and provisions, but they forgot to walk in His principles. Like Adam and Eve, we are designed with God's DNA which represents His spiritual computer chip that created us in His likeness with spiritual receptors that allow us to live on earth and still communicate with our heavenly Father. You may ask if spiritual receptors were created over two thousand years ago, how do we know they still operate? My answer is that I talked to the Father this morning, and so did many of you. For in Him we live, we move, and we have our being. The first evidence of your greatness to God is revealed in His unconditional love for you because God is love! He gives us reminders like, *"Before I formed you in the womb, I knew you." [Jeremiah 1:5]*; *"Before the foundation of the world, you were loved in Christ our Lord and Savior." [John 17:24]*; *"Greater love has no man than this, that he lay down his life for his friends." [John 15:13].* Now that is exactly what Christ did for all people including you and me.

One of the greatest treatises on God's unconditional, agape love is written in [1st. Corinthians 13:4-8] which exemplifies the God-kind of love that He desires for us to replicate in our daily living since we have His spiritual DNA. *"Love suffers long and is kind; love does not envy; love does not parade itself, is not puffed up; does not behave rudely, does not seek its own, is not provoked, thinks no evil; does not rejoice in iniquity, but rejoices in the truth; bears all things, believes all things, hopes all things, endures all things. Love never fails."* NKJV

Some people have a different concept of love than previously described. Love to some is determined by a response to their needs, wishes, and every desire. Many believe that love should afford them status, power, or simply handouts to pay the rent or monthly mortgage. I can assure you that God is the only one who will love you in spite of who you are or what you have.

God's love for you is not based on what you have, but who you are. His love is not contingent on the kind of car you drive, the bills you owe, the job you have or don't have, the house you live in, nor the amount of money in your bank account. Jesus loves you for who you are. He doesn't condone sin, but He loves the individual unconditionally in that He desires a relationship with you and me because we are part of God's family. We are described as, *"A chosen generation, a royal priesthood. A holy nation, His own special people, that you may proclaim the praises of Him who called you out of darkness into His marvelous light."* [1st Peter 2:9] At the time of salvation, we put on royalty, and we became His righteousness through the shed blood of Jesus Christ, God's only begotten Son.

Another example of your greatness in God's eyesight is that God designed you to have dominion and power in order to rule and reign over His earthly kingdom. His desire is for us to live on earth as it is in heaven. You were created to be Satan's master, not his slave. He was not meant to have authority over our schools, our family, or this nation. *"So God created man in his own image; in the image of God He created Him; male and female, He created them. Then God blessed them and God said to them, be fruitful, and multiply; fill the earth and subdue it; have dominion over the fish of the sea, over the birds of the air and, every living thing that moves on the earth."* [Genesis 1:27-28]

Adam and Eve decided to disobey God's command to eat of every fruit bearing tree in the Garden of Eden except the tree of the knowledge of good and evil. Through disobedience man gave the earthly kingdom to Satan. The law became their slave master to teach them right from wrong. However, man could not keep the law; to break one law is the same as breaking them all. After six failed covenants, God revealed the mystery that had been hidden in Jesus Christ. Through faith in Christ, His death, burial and resurrection, we received redemptive authority to regain fellowship with God.

Again, let me remind you that you are someone who is very special to God! He designed you to defeat the enemy. You have been restored to a place of power and dominion without the curse of the law. God's grace is sufficient to set you free by your confession of faith in the finished work of Jesus Christ who gave his life so that we might live. Now, that man is no longer under Satan's rule, we have become friends with our heavenly Father and nothing can separate us from Him. Our spiritual receptors via the Holy Spirit are the power sources that continue to make this connection possible.

"Who shall separate us from the love of Christ? Shall tribulation, persecution, or famine, nakedness, peril or sword? As it is written: For your sake, we are killed all day long; we are counted as sheep for the slaughter. Yet in all these things we are more than conquerors through Him who loved us. For I am persuaded that neither death nor life, nor angels nor principalities nor powers, nor things present nor things to come nor height nor depth, nor any created thing shall be able to separate us from the love of God which is in Christ Jesus our Lord." [Romans 8:35-39] NKJV

Your level of happiness or loneliness is also important to God. Although happiness is considered to be based on one's feelings and emotions at any given moment, joy has a different function. Joy is an inborn state of being that you received at salvation. Joy is part of the born-again experience that one has due to a conversion experience from the old man to the new. You are never alone in that you are sealed with the Holy Spirit as your Comforter. The first time the Holy Spirit revealed Himself to a group was on the day of Pentecost, fifty days after the resurrection of Christ. He is the third person of the Godhead. God has given us His power to be a witness to His presence in the world today.

You have been designed with greatness to prosper even as your soul prospers. There are several areas in which God wants you to prosper. God wants you to prosper in your health. Would you want your child to be sick? Well, neither does God want you to be sick. Sickness does not glorify God. You are not "just suffering for the Lord" unless you are being persecuted for sharing the Gospel of Jesus Christ to save the multitudes like the Apostle Paul. The cross on which Christ suffered and died also bought the right for you and me to be healed. Surely, He has borne our grief and carried our sorrows and by His stripes, we were healed.

God wants you to prosper in your soul which includes your mind, will, and emotions. You received a new Spirit filled with an awareness of God's presence when you were reborn, but your soulish realm did not change. That is to say that your soul, which is your mind, emotions and desires still want the same things after salvation as it did before salvation. The Holy Spirit is our helper who desires to bring change if we allow Him to operate in areas of weakness. When the soul prospers, our entire life will prosper. Although God destined us for greatness, many believers will never attain it. Those individuals who live according to their sinful nature have their minds set on what their flesh desires, but those who live according to the Spirit, have their minds set on what the Spirit desires. Only if you live in the Spirit will you be able to deny the lusts of the flesh. The mind controlled by sinful acts brings death, but the mind controlled by the Spirit is life and peace.

There is a big difference between the carnal Christian and the Christian who lives according to the Spirit. The carnal believer is hostile to God and cannot win at life because of double-mindedness. The carnal Christian will remain immature until he or she desires to change. Change comes only with focused intensity and with the help of the Holy Spirit. The carnal believer may remain immature in the things of God for many years even though it is not intentional. The problem is that they will not gain power over their circumstances because they are dead to God's blessings and provisions. When you talk to people without vision, they make excuses for their malfunction by blaming others, their past, and they even blame God.

On the other hand, those who live according to the Spirit will prosper in their mind. They have set their mind on changing, and they believe what God's Word said about the situation. They set their faces like flit until they receive the manifestation of their petition or prayer request. The prosperous soul has several characteristics:

1. The prosperous soul says I am blessed and highly favored. Everything I touch will be blessed.

2. The prosperous soul believes in tithing as heaven's economic system.

3. They believe that God will open up the windows of heaven and pour out a blessing in their time of need.

4. They read, pray, and meditate on God's Word daily.

5. They eagerly give to help others out of the overflow of their abundance.

When you change your thinking, you allow the mind of Christ in you to take you from good to great! Renewing your mind is mandatory in order to prosper in any area of your life. New thought patterns must be practiced until they are automatic. It takes twenty-one repetitions of an action before it becomes a habit. When you become committed to change, submit that situation to the authority of the Holy Spirit as it is very difficult to change successfully on your own.

As a result of your growth in the mind of Christ, instead of feeling hurt, He will say forgive; instead of living in fear; He says have faith in God; Instead of giving up, know that He is the God of a second chance. Instead of criticizing and judging others, He says they are a work in progress just like you!

You have been designed with eternal security in Jesus Christ, our savior and soon coming King. *"But God who is rich in mercy, because of His great love with which he loved us, even when we were dead in trespasses made us alive together with Christ and raised us up together, and made us sit in heavenly places in Christ Jesus."* [Ephesians 2:4-6] NKJV

Through Christ we stand acquitted, not guilty before God. Before salvation, man was dead in his sins, but by God's grace through faith, we have been forgiven. In Christ, there is no longer a spirit of bondage since we have received the Spirit of adoption into God's family. The Holy Spirit bears witness with our spirit that we are children of God and also joint-heirs with Jesus Christ.

We are no longer slaves; we are the Master's children with the same privileges as sons of the Most High. You have already received the best that heaven has to offer; God's son, Jesus, His forgiveness, and eternal life if you are a born-again believer. Whosoever will receive Jesus as their Lord and savior will enjoy these same benefits of salvation.

As believers in Christ, you have been designed for greatness whether you believe it or not. Jesus loves you, and He will never leave you alone. Jesus loves you so much that if you fall, He will continue to pull you out of your miry clay of sin, destructive behaviors, anger, bitterness, addictions, and poor choices. He will stretch you until you stop making excuses and having pity parties.

God is love. He is not angry with you. He is a God of purpose who wants us to receive the awesome plan He has for our lives. Jesus was obedient to His Father until death. A holy lifestyle pleases God in that you will be blessed to produce much fruit for the kingdom until He comes.

I am convinced that until you can believe in God's description of who you are, and in what He says you can have, you will live a life of low self-esteem, fear, insufficiency, feeling hurt and rejected, and without the power and confidence to see fruit in your life. What makes people live in mediocrity and stagnation? I have a few suggestions:

1. Fear and doubt
2. Unbelief
3. Complacency
4. Sin
5. Pride

Again, I feel the need to remind you that God designed you for greatness in every area of your life. You have been made righteous in Christ, and you have been created in His image with His nature, and His character. You have been given dominion and power to rule and reign over His earthly kingdom. You are designed to prosper in all things, in health, and wealth even as your soul prospers. You have eternal security in the spiritual kingdom because the Word records that you are already a joint-heir with Jesus

Christ, and in Him you are already seated in heavenly places as evidenced by the power of His resurrection.

Be determined to move on to maturity in the plan God has for your life as a witness of salvation. Please know that inaction is also disobedience. I believe you are someone's miracle about to happen today; you are someone's word of wisdom to cause a mighty harvest to come forth; you are the light that can dispel darkness in someone's life today; You can be the oil of joy for a mourning soul today if only you will decide to believe that God designed you to magnify His greatness!

Father God, my prayer is that we will come into the knowledge of who you predestined us to be. You have not given us a spirit of fear, but of power, love, and a sound mind. You have given us dominion and have made us more than conquerors. There is no one like You; all creation call you God. You have translated us from a world of darkness into your marvelous light. We have been justified and made righteous by your grace. Let your light burn in us until we attain the nature and character of Christ with the indwelling power of the Holy Spirit. Amen!

"Now may the God of peace Himself sanctify you completely; and may your whole spirit, soul, and body be preserved blameless at the coming of the Lord Jesus Christ."

[1 Thessalonians 5:23]

Two

PREDESTINED FOR VICTORY: SPIRIT, SOUL, AND BODY

God has predestined you for victory in every area of your life. The victorious life that was predestined for us by God includes physical and emotional healing. It is important for us to understand what God has made available to His children. We live in His presence as part of creation, but it is our choice to believe in His principles which will determine the quality and longevity of life for each individual. We have been predestined to live in divine health. Our health is important to God.

There was no sickness in the garden until disobedience entered into the minds of Adam and Eve. Most often, prolonged sickness is a curse. God intended for us to live in optimum health. Just like Satan beguiled Adam and Eve, he desires to inflict pain and suffering on the lives of believers and to make them think it's all right to be sick or depressed. A transfer of power also took place. When Adam violated God's command, the authority God gave Adam allowed Satan to become the god of this world, and he brought with him everything that steals, kills, and destroys.

Adam's sin caused sickness, disease and death to enter the world. Spiritual death was followed by physical death, and mental disorders. Adam was supposed to live forever; however, longevity for mankind ranged from 930 years, to 120 years, then from 90 to about 70 years or less today due to sickness. This is happening to some believers because of the idea that doctors have all the answers. The side effects of many prescriptions may kill the patient before the desired healing becomes effective. This doesn't have to happen in the body of Christ. If we believe God's Word, we will be free from sickness and disease. We should also know in advance when we will die because the Holy Spirit will show us things to come. *Amen! [John: 16:13]*

We live in His presence without relying on the provisions already appropriated to us through the shed blood of Christ. Medicine is one choice, but faith in God for a total recovery is the best alternative in that medicine will no longer be needed. God is always expecting us to line up with His Word. We just need to receive what has already been promised to us. Healing was provided for us long before we needed it. God didn't invent a cure when you became sick. He provided for our healing before we were born.

"Surely He has borne our grief and carried our sorrows: yet we esteemed Him stricken, smitten of God, and afflicted. But He was wounded for our transgressions; He was bruised for our iniquities: the chastisement of our peace was upon Him; and with His stripes we are healed." [Isaiah 53:4-5]

Jesus' earthly ministry was centered around healing the sick. He never told anyone that their case was too difficult for Him. He didn't call in the family and pronounce the number of days or months the person had left before death. Jesus healed every person who came to Him for healing no matter what was wrong with them. If you are sick, you need to go to God and ask Him to heal you as He instructed us to do. If you have faith in God's Word and not doubt, you will always receive your healing.

If God said it, He is able to perform it. I had to take that attitude to receive my healing several years ago. I had to put a strong demand on my faith, pray, and meditate on the Word day and night. I had received a medical diagnosis that degenerative, bulging discs, and pinched nerves in the spinal cord were the reasons for the severe trauma I endured every day all day. After a year of therapy with no results, I sought out a neurological surgeon who informed me that my situation would result in several operations over the years to replace worn out discs. The cost was also far above my medical insurance limits which would require me to spend most of my savings. After my diagnosis, the doctor asked me not to take more than a week or two to decide when I wanted to schedule my operation because the lower section of my spine had already decayed in my back.

Needless to say, I was faced with the most trying dilemma of my entire life. My thoughts were centered around the fact that I had already missed too many days from work, my youngest son needed more of my time now that his father had recently gone home to be with the Lord, and my other two sons, in college at the time, expected their monthly deposits for college expenses. I made a final decision to postpone the operation for now. However, that didn't last long when I discovered that I couldn't drive at times, nor could I sit down due to the intense, excruciating pain in my back. I had to stand up all day while I taught my classes, and I had to walk around while eating my lunch because bending to sit was very difficult. Finally, I gave in to the pain, and I drove directly to the doctor's office to schedule my operation, but it was too late. The receptionist informed me that my doctor had recently died in a car accident . She thought I knew this and that I only came by to pick up my X-Rays.

That day I stopped looking for a surgeon, but I found my healer, Jesus Christ. I did what most people do. I looked for a quick fix rather than a total recovery. I began to do what I now advocate to those who are sick. First, realize that sickness and disease are usually curses from the enemy and not blessings from God. Jesus defeated every curse of the devil, and triumphed over every sin and all sickness when he sacrificed His life for us on the cross. We have the victory if we would only believe. In the natural, I could visualize myself sitting in a royal blue wheelchair trying to support my family, but spiritually I knew that my healing DNA was connected to my God who promised that He would never leave me nor forsake me.

My healing was a process that led me to great intimacy with the Holy Spirit and the Word of God. The Bible became my textbook which I read from cover to cover several times. I wanted to know everything about Jesus' healing ministry. I began to meditate on several healing scriptures to the point of writing them on index cards so that when the pain became unbearable, I would pull them from my purse and read them over and over, faster and faster until the pain began to subside. As I look back on those days, it brings tears to my eyes when I realize that God was doing a lot more than teaching me about healing. He was bringing me into a deeper relationship by teaching me how to depend on Him in everything. The following list of healing scripture references reveal that God does not show partiality toward people who seek healing. Faith is the master key. If God has healed before, He is able to heal again and again and again until you learn that He is the Lord, our healer.

"Then Peter opened his mouth and said: In truth I perceive that God shows no partiality. But in every nation whoever fears (respects) Him and works righteousness is accepted by Him."[Acts 10:34-35]

"Have faith in God. For assuredly, I say to you whoever says to this mountain, be removed and be cast into the sea; and does not doubt in his heart, but believes that those things he says will be done, he will have whatever he says. Therefore I say to you, whatever things you ask when you pray, believe that you receive them and you will have them." [Mark 11: 23-24]

"For He was wounded for our transgressions, and He was bruised for our iniquities ... and by His stripes you are healed." [Isaiah 53:5]

"And Jesus went about all Galilee, teaching in their synagogues preaching the gospel of the kingdom, and healing all kinds of sickness and all kinds of disease among the people. Then His fame went throughout all Syria; and they brought to Him all sick people who were afflicted with various diseases and torments, and those who were demon-possessed, epileptics, and paralytics; and he healed them." [Matthew 4:23, 24]

"How God anointed Jesus of Nazareth with the Holy Spirit and with power, who went about doing good and healing all who were oppressed by the devil, for God was with Him." [Acts 10:38]

"...For I am the Lord who heals you." [Exodus 15:26]

"Who Himself bore our sins in His own body on the tree, that we, having died to sin, might live for righteousness-by whose stripes you were healed." [1Peter 2:24]

Several other scriptures along with many Bible references about people being healed are used to give evidence that Jesus is our healer. Many months passed as I immersed myself in the Word with prayer and meditation many times during the day. My health continued to deteriorate, but my spirit was growing stronger. I confessed that I was already healed because I knew without a doubt that God would heal me. It was a matter of time. I no longer focused on the pain, but how it would feel to be healed.

I developed a compassionate, loving relationship with Christ during those two years, then one morning the Holy Spirit said, "Stand up straight; you are healed!" At first I didn't believe it. I continued to walk sideways as I had done for so long to avoid the pain. I don't know why I ignored that voice after waiting almost two years for my healing, but I found myself bending over and moving around like nothing was wrong that day. It finally hit me that evening that I was indeed healed with no pain at all. The running, yelling, and screaming frightened my son as I ran around the house shouting praises to God like a wild person. This is the short version of my story, and I can say after twenty plus years, I am still healed with absolutely no back pain whatever. Praise the Lord! We have the victory in Christ if we only trust and obey His Word. My question to those who believe that sickness is of God is this, if God wants you to suffer for the Lord, then why do you take the doctor's medicine to get well?

It is God's will for us to be healed physically and mentally, for we have the "mind of Christ." The enemy doesn't want you to have balance in mind, spirit, and body which is considered wholeness. The devil doesn't want you to know the power you possess over him through the blood of Jesus. He knows that when you really know who you are, you can walk in the full embodiment of Christ with the authority of the Godhead operating on your behalf and triumph over him. When you understand the voice of victory you have in Christ, you will stand invincible, against depression, Bi-polar disorder, diabetes, cancer, and other illnesses that will no longer have control over you. Resist the devil by speaking faith-filled words, and he will have to flee. God wants you to have a breakthrough, not a breakdown!

Our Lord and Savior, Jesus Christ, shed His precious blood in seven places so that you and I would receive healing. The thirty-nine stripes on Jesus' back won back our health. His sweat like drops of blood in the Garden of Gethesemane paid for our victory over Satan. He was bruised (inner bleeding) for our iniquities (inherited moral weakness) now we don't have to pass them on to our children. The crown of thorns on his head, (a sign of poverty) paid the price for the curse of poverty. The nails in his hands paid for our inheritance and authority in His name. The nails in His feet paid the price for our peace; He will never leave you nor forsake you. The spear in His side where blood and water flowed paid the price to heal the brokenhearted. Jesus heals the sick because of His love, His mercy, and His compassion toward us.

He healed us spiritually, physically, and psychologically. Below are some steps to take to receive your healing:

Make sure there is no sin in your life.

Read scriptures that empower your faith.

Be prepared to stand on those scriptures in faith until healing manifests.

Speak –up and say, "By His stripes I am healed."

Release your faith continually.

See yourself already healed.

Be prepared to believe that you receive.

Praise and worship and listen to healing CD's.

Begin to thank God for the victory in advance.

A Victorious Mind

You have also been predestined to have victory over thoughts, and behaviors that don't line up with the Word of God. Our spirit was instantly transformed after receiving salvation, but the mind did not change. Many Christians make little progress beyond conversion. They are God's children, but they continue to do the same things they did before salvation. It was very puzzling to me when

I was younger and even today, to see church members grow older without changing the way they think or act. I finally realized what was wrong. It takes effort and focused intensity to change; consequently, most people are simply content to live in God's presence and enjoy His provisions, without living by His principles. This hallmark scripture says it all:

"And so dear brothers and sisters, I plead with you to give your bodies to God because of all He has done for you. Let them be a living sacrifice –the kind He will find acceptable . This is truly the way to worship Him. Don't copy the behaviors and customs of the world , but let God transform you into a new person by changing the way you think. Then you will learn God's will for you, which is good and pleasing and perfect." [Romans 12:1-2] NLT

Arthur Fletcher's phrase, "A mind is a terrible thing to waste," is a phrase that not only applies to those with educational challenges, but also to those with spiritual challenges as well. We need our minds to think, learn, remember, understand, imagine and to make choices. The mind determines your actions -how you live, how you behave and conduct yourself. When you were born again, by the grace of God, you received a brand new spirit; however, your mind was not completely renewed. Your mind has to be reprogrammed to line-up with God's Word. As born-again children of God, we are expected to think, speak, and live according to the character of Christ. We are to put on the new man, and no longer walk in the carnal desires of the old nature.

Many Christians make very little if any progress beyond becoming born again. They may stop smoking, drinking, and they may attend church, but there is very little internal change of their desires, thoughts, and feelings or mind-set. This internal change will only come with the help of the Holy Spirit and your decision to change. Churches are full of baby Christians who are not learning, growing, or maturing in God's Word; as a result, they are miserable and depressed, and often they will blame God for their circumstances and the pit in which they find themselves. The Word of God must be acted upon in order to bring transformation to the weak areas of our lives.

Your mind will not be renewed automatically just because you became a Christian. Change involves being a doer of the Word. After reading and hearing the truth of God's Word, it is important to diligently practice what the Word says in order to have victory in your daily living. Many Christian learn about conquering their debt problem, having a successful relationship with their spouse, eating right to solve their weight problem, but if they never apply what was learned, there will be no metamorphosis or transformation from the old to the new.

The Bible says that as a man thinks, so is his life. Satan knows that thoughts lead to action; that's why he desires to fill your mind with strongholds of lust, fear, offense, rejection, and low self-worth so that you will not have victory on earth as God intended. Satan wants to fill your mind with vain impressions and images that lead you away from meditating on God's Word. Satan wants to make you question God by infiltrating your mind with intellectual reasoning such as philosophy, false teachings, scientific principles, and other intellectual ideas that create doubt and rejection of the Christian faith.

Wrong thoughts will lock you into poverty, depression, worry, sickness and other crippling, ineffective works of the devil. These behaviors will not change on their own. The key to transforming the mind is to meditate on the Word until it becomes part of your daily schedule. You have to set your mind like you set your clock. Change requires a focused intensity to take every thought and behavior captive until you conquer that thing with the help of the Holy Spirit. It takes twenty-one repeated actions to form a new habit. For example, if I want to stop speaking negative words about how much I hate my job, I have to retract wrong words the minute they are spoken 21 plus times before I can retrain myself from one negative thought pattern.

The soul of a man is made up of the mind, the will, and the emotions. Your spirit, which is the real you, is the part that was born-again and made you a righteous, new spirit created in the image of God. Neither your soul nor your body was changed when you accepted Christ. That is why your mind becomes the battlefield where the victory in life will be won or lost. Salvation of the spirit comes at your confession and acceptance of Christ as your Lord and savior. Transformation of the soul is a long-term growth process. *James 1:21 says, "Therefore lay aside all filthiness, and overflow of wickedness, and receive with meekness the implanted word, which is able to save your souls."*

God designed our minds to learn His ways in order to see victory in this life on earth and throughout eternity, "as it is in heaven." *"For those who live according to the flesh, set their minds on the things of the flesh, but those who live according to the Spirit, the things of the Spirit. For to be carnally minded is death, but to be spiritually minded is life and peace." [Romans 8:5-6]* This verse shows us that the mind decides if we live in the flesh, which is our sin nature, or if we live in the Spirit, which is the Godly, recreated part of the Christian. The things you set your mind on will soon become your behavior.

Statistics prove that if a child watches violent cartoons, he will become agitated and aggressive. Likewise, if a person watches pornographic movies, the desire for sexual fantasies will increase. On the other hand, if you read and meditate on the scriptures, you will desire an intimacy with Christ. What kind of death is Romans 8:5-6 speaking of? Spiritual death does not mean a loss of salvation. The kind of death referred to by Paul, is the separation from the blessings and the provisions of God. When you focus on materialistic desires, thoughts of anger, frustration, and violence, your peace and the life you could have is cut off from God. Although God has predestined you and me for victory, we have to choose to receive it.

Any effort to transform your thoughts can be a real challenge if you are determined to change your present "comfort zone." When I began to learn the difference between carnality and Christianity, I realized why so many Christians had remained the same. Many Christians continue the same pattern of going to church Sunday after Sunday, but they still complain all week long about their jobs, not having enough money, or about some physical ailments. After reading through the Bible and listening to a few good teachers of my day, I realized that living in the peace and joy of a kingdom lifestyle here on earth meant change. As I began to rely more on godly principles than my own reality, the Holy Spirit began a new work in me.

Changing my thoughts and words took many months if not years of intense work. I began to gain some control over my speaking even if I had to replace a negative statement immediately with a positive one. When I had a desire for nicotine, I would say that I can do all things through Christ who strengthens me. If my finances were low, I repeated scriptures that spoke of having my needs met such as:

"And my God shall supply all my needs according to His riches in glory by Christ Jesus." [Philippians 4:19] , or "Because he has set his love on Me, therefore I will deliver him; I will set him on high, because he has known My name. He shall call upon Me and I will answer him; I will be with him in trouble; I will deliver him and honor him." Psalm 91:14-15]

As I began to draw closer to God, He began to show me that He is faithful, and that He honors His Word above His name. [Psalm 138:2] NKJV I can remember many times when I had to put these words of scripture to the test. I had begun to refuse to say that I don't have money, or I can't buy that. I heard a pastor say in a service once that if I were a tither, I could draw on my heavenly bank account in times of need. One day this theory was put to the test. I went to lunch with my co-workers even though I knew my funds were insufficient to cover my meal. Nevertheless, I really believed that God would supply my needs. My co-workers placed their orders while I stepped out of line to speak to someone. I returned to the line and began to think of what I would order.

I decided to put an even greater demand on my trust in God's word than ever. I ordered hors d'oeuvres for our table, and one of the most expensive entrées on the menu. I remember smiling as the cashier gave me the total. I made a motion to look in my purse for the money which in the natural, I knew would not be there, but I was relying on my spiritual bank account to manifest which is my faith in God. The cashier looked at my ticket and said, " Your order has been paid." I asked if he were sure, and he said that he was positive.

My faith and trust in God astounded me that day as I learned that if you have the faith to believe it, then God has the power to perform it! Our DNA receptors teach us to practice setting our mind on the things of God, not the things of the world. When you choose to control your mind, you can attain the destiny God has designed for your life. After that experience, my faith went to another level. When I start to worry about lack and insufficiency, I am reminded that:

"He shall be like a tree planted by the rivers of water, that brings forth its fruit in its season, whose leaf also shall not wither; and whatever he does shall prosper." [Psalm 1:3] I know God cares about His children even more than we know how to care for our own. For example, the Book of Genesis gives an account of how God told Abraham to sacrifice his precious son, Isaac. Abraham obeyed God, but at the last minute, Abraham was told not to harm his son. Abraham totally trusted God who provided him a ram for the sacrifice. Abraham named that place Jehovah-Jireh, which means God will provide. God has predestined you for victory even when time seems limited.

The next time you need His help, remember that your circumstances should not dictate your position; you are more than a conqueror. Your situation is not your birthright unless it proclaims the promise God has for you. You may be in the habit of expecting less, but God doesn't. Refuse to let your personal problems defeat your purpose in life. You may be walking in the valley right now, but God has prepared a feast for you in the midst of your enemies. Again, Don't breakdown! Breakthrough to victory in every area of your life!

The mind needs training and exercise like the physical body in order to change. Nothing gets better on its own. Everything left to itself decays, declines, and loses the momentum to function at an optimum level. When Joshua needed a Word from the Lord, he was reminded that God had already predestined him for victory. He had to remember God's promises.

"This book of the law(God's Word) shall not depart from your mouth, but you shall meditate on it day and night, that you may observe to do according to all that is written in it. For then YOU will make your way prosperous, and then YOU will have good success." [Joshua 1:8]

In this passage of scripture, Joshua was taking over leadership of the nation of Israel, and God was giving him instructions for this difficult task. The key to his success was to keep God's Word in his mouth and in his mind. If he did this, God promised him victory and prosperity.

On the other hand, if Joshua had filled his mind and his mouth with words of fear, negative speaking, worry and doubt, he would have failed without receiving the promises of the Lord. It amazes me that many Christians speak negative, doubtful words that hinder God from performing the intended miracle. They kill their seed before it germinates and blame God or the devil for their disappointment when the Word says *that "Death and life are in the power of the tongue, and those who love it will eat its fruit." [Proverbs 18:21]* To experience God's promises, we must renew our minds with God's way of thinking and speaking.

Our flesh does not want to leave its comfort zone. If we let the flesh lead us, which is a way of thinking that oppose God's words, we will oversleep every day, have a bad attitude, and do wrong things. If we are born again, our spirit is in agreement with God. The flesh was originally created in the image of God, but from the time Adam and Eve sinned in the Garden of Eden until now, the flesh has been bound by the ways of Satan. The devil works through the fleshly realm by causing our minds to agree with our flesh; consequently, the carnal mind is an enemy to God and a friend of the devil.

What God wants us to think or meditate on ministers life. *"Finally, brethren, whatever things are true, whatever things are noble, whatever things are just, whatever things are pure, whatever things are lovely, whatever things are of good report, if there be any virtue and if there is anything praiseworthy, meditate on these things."* [Philippians 4:8] NKJV

Satan, the god of this world, wants to keep you ignorant and mentally anorexic so that he can cause you to remain deprived of the destiny preordained by God through faith in Christ. You have to change your thoughts from a self-defeating mind-set to a solution focused mind-set that speaks the solution to the problem instead of rehearsing the problem.

We claim to be Christians who are filled with the mind of Christ on Sunday. What we must realize is that Jesus wants to be involved in every part of every aspect of our lives which includes our day to day prayer and worship during the entire week. Focus on these five key concepts to reset your mind for victory.

❖

Victorious Concepts

1. Salvation or the new birth instantly changed your spirit. Your soul (mind will, and emotions/feelings), will not

change until you take thoughts, feelings, and emotions captive and commit to change as you become more knowledgeable of God's Word. This is a process that extends over many years. Living a life of wholeness means that your spirit, soul and body should operate together as one.

"Now may the God of peace Himself sanctify you completely; and may your whole spirit, soul, and body be preserved blameless at the coming of our Lord Jesus Christ." [1st Thessalonians 5:23]

2. You can be on your way to heaven, but live in hell on earth if you refuse to obey what the Bible teaches. Many believers will live in God's presence having been born again with His DNA, but they will defy His principles or His Word. We have to choose to live God's way which brings love, joy, and peace in the Holy Spirit, or the way of Satan which brings fear, poverty, and death. Jesus demonstrated the importance and effectiveness of knowing and applying scripture to combat temptation from the enemy by saying, "It is written" and we should do the same! Amen?

3. Renewing the mind is a life-style, not a one- time experience. Be aware of how you think and feel when things don't go your way. Then, practice thoughts and words that imitate what Jesus would say until they become your own. Many people who say they are Christians expect God to change their carnal ways while He is waiting for them to grow up so that He can use them to build His earthly kingdom. Change in one area does not mean we have success in another area. Renewing the mind means making a conscious effort to change.

"And do not be conformed to this world, but be transformed by the renewing of your mind, that you may prove what is that good and acceptable, and perfect will of God." [Romans 12:2]

4. Allow the Holy Spirit to help you change by practicing God's thoughts and words. Notice how a doctor or lawyer will spend time and money to acquire the skills to do their job successfully. They will follow a certain regiment every day, and they will submit to a board of directors until they qualify for the job. Christians should also want to commit time to daily prayer and meditation to do the job they are called to do.

5. Taking off the old man is as important as putting on the new man. The Bible says, *"That you put off, concerning your former conduct, the old man which grows corrupt according to the deceitful lusts, and be renewed in the spirit of your mind, and that you put on the new man which was created according to God, in true righteousness and holiness." [Ephesians 4:22-24]*

Your life will not prosper until your soul-mind, will, and emotions prosper. God's word is the final authority in all the issues of life. Your soul connects your spirit and body. Your thoughts come from your soul. Your thoughts direct your decisions, actions, and feelings every day. The Holy Spirit speaks to your spirit, not to your head; that's why you can live as a spiritual being that communicates with God and also function in the natural world. Your soul is different from your spirit. You can be a born again Christian, but struggle with finances, your marriage, family members, and other issues of life because your soul has not been renewed or changed from your old ways of thinking and acting. The degree that you renew your mind will determine the amount of health, wealth, and peace you experience in life. Your entire church may need to be taught that victory depends on mind renewal.

There were certain things I had never heard about victorious living until years later. I didn't know that tithing was God's prosperity principle until I purposed to test it. Every promise of God has to operate by faith or it will not work. I had to learn healing scriptures and say by His stripes, I am healed even though my back was in pain. I was speaking healing by faith until the manifestation came. I realized that God doesn't want to punish anyone with sickness because He loves us. Why seek help from doctors if He wants you to be sick? Or why work every day, sometimes two or three jobs, if He wants you to hate prosperity? We must remove every thought that is contrary to believing God; otherwise, we will live in his presence, but struggle with our own religious reality. *"You shall love the Lord your God with all your heart, with all your soul, and with all your mind." [Matthew 22:37]* He commands the entire person to love Him. Every part must line-up with His Word as we mature in the mind of Christ.

The converted, prosperous soul has several characteristics such as:

- A readiness to repent and to change any thoughts or attitude to conform to what God's Word says at any time. [Romans 12:2]

- A willingness to follow the Holy Spirit, not the flesh_ *"For those who live according to the flesh set their minds on the things of the flesh, but those who live according to the Spirit, the things of the Spirit. For to be carnally minded is death, but to be spiritually minded is life and peace." [Romans 8:5-6]*

- A desire to meditate on God's Word daily_ *"But his delight is the law of the Lord, and in His law he meditates day and night." [Psalm 1:2]*

- Disciplined to do positive things without fear or worry_ *"You will keep him in perfect peace, whose mind is stayed on You." [Isaiah 26:3]*

- Determine to do God's will no matter what it costs- *"And if it seems evil to you to serve the Lord, choose for yourselves this day whom you will serve, whether the gods which your fathers served that were on the other side of the River, or the gods of the Amorites, in whose land you dwell. But as for me and my house, we will serve the Lord." [Joshua 24:15]*

- Be eager to follow the direction of the Holy Spirit_ *"For as many as are led by the Spirit of God, these are sons of God." [Romans 8:14]*

- Be established and disciplined in the Word of God rather than being controlled by emotions and feelings_" For we walk by faith, not by sight." [2nd Corinthians 5:7]

- Be sanctified, pure, and free from unclean thoughts and behavior. Think on these things... [Philippians 4:8]

Victory steps for growth will not come until you make a commitment to change with the help of the Holy Spirit. The following basic steps for change may be used as a guide:

1. FIRST, BELIEVE YOU CAN CHANGE. Other people are not the problem. Refrain from blame-shifting and be responsible for your own actions. If you want a better life, it is up to you to change in the realm of your mind, will, and emotions.

2. PROGRAM YOUR THINKING. Use positive self-talk and positive self-affirmations. Positive self-talk will help to develop an optimistic outlook whereby you can expect positive things to happen.

3. MAKE A DECISION TO CHANGE. Trying to change is not change. You know what needs to be changed better than anyone else. Some believers still struggle with fornication, adultery, drugs, pornography, lying, stealing and the list goes on. The Holy Spirit will bring on a conviction which lets you know your secret sins can no longer be tolerated because God wants to use you for His glory. God loves the person, but hates the sin.

4. REPLACE CRITICAL, JUDGMENTAL, AND CONTROLLING SPIRITS WITH ENCOURAGEMENT. Instead of focusing on the negativism in yourself and others, replace those thoughts with words of exhortation. Compliment yourself and those around you by speaking of things that have already been accomplished.

5. FOCUS ON WHAT YOU CAN DO, NOT ON WHAT YOU CAN'T DO. Avoid the "I can't..." quagmire. Make positive, uplifting remarks. Start to believe that your Heavenly Father's DNA established in you dominion and authority. Now that those holy receptors are functioning again, focus on what YOU are able to do, NOT WHAT OTHERS ARE ABLE TO DO FOR YOU!

6. MAKE A DECISION TO BE A WINNER IN EVERY AREA OF YOUR LIFE! There was a forty year old man who earned a weekly salary of forty dollars. He realized that time was moving rapidly in his career, so he came up with an inspiring plan on how to mass produce the automobile. Twenty years later he was the richest man in the world. His name was Henry Ford.

Another young man used his talents to write and produce plays that were first performed in restaurants. He could not pay the rent which forced him to live in his car. He spoke of eating cookies for many meals while writing his plays. This young man is now a billionaire and one of the richest producers in Hollywood. His name is Tyler Perry. If our minds are not trained and taught how to think with the mind of Christ, we will be the same twenty years from now. We have to choose to think right thoughts daily.

Be aware of behaviors that will hinder a renewed mind such as:

- ANGER will prevent positive thoughts and could produce thoughts of hatred or revenge that can be harmful to yourself and others.

- UNFORGIVENESS is toxic. Be wise enough to forgive those who have hurt you. Forgiveness is a gift you give yourself to gain freedom from bondage.

- MURMURING AND COMPLAINING will destroy harmony and can bring about unnecessary pain and suffering.

- POOR COMMUNICATION can hinder progress and send mixed messages to others. Good communication brings understandings and builds a foundation for healthy relationships. If one person refuses to discuss mutual concerns with the other, walls of confusion and misunderstanding develop causing resentment and rejection. Problems don't get better if they are left unresolved no matter how much time elapses. Time only heals wounds that have been addressed.

Some of the most fundamental problems that affect mankind are feelings of inadequacy, worthlessness, and feeling useless. We are our own worst critics. It's time to do some cognitive-restructuring which means to trace negative thoughts back to their origin in order to investigate and replace maladaptive thinking that trigger irrational responses. If there is no Godly premise for such thoughts, cast them out and speak what the Word says about that situation.

I am here to tell you that you were created to be a person of vision, and to live a healthy and prosperous life. You may feel like the master of defeat, but the Word of God says this:

" You are a chosen generation, a royal priesthood, a holy nation, His own special people, that you may proclaim the praises of Him who called you out of darkness into His marvelous light,

who once were not a people, but are now the people of God, who had not obtained mercy, but now have obtained mercy." [1st Peter 2:9-10]

❖

A Victorious Self-Image

Living in God's presence gives you victory over your self-worth. You have been adopted into God's family and raised up with Christ to sit in heavenly places. You can't let Satan steal your self-worth. He desires to steal, kill, and destroy every dream you will ever have for yourself, your children, or your business. God gave us the place of importance that Satan has always wanted. Naturally, he will try to talk you into becoming a shy, introverted individual who delays your walking in the principles of courage, strength, and power.

A negative belief-system can start very early in life. Most negative messages that influence one's low self-image were planted as early as elementary school. As a child, I bet you were energetic, creative, very intelligent, and excited about life until you met these three fears that became a part of your belief-system as you continued to grow. They are: 1) Fear of rejection, 2) Fear of change, and 3) Fear of success. These fears or phobias can lead to roadblocks that cause Failure reinforcement (always looking back at failure), and Failure forecasting (looking forward to failure in the future). Other people, family, events in life, and one's environment may influence the way you see yourself, but ultimately YOU have the greatest influence over the image you have of yourself.

The way you view yourself deep in the heart of your personality determines who you will become in life. Charles Swindoll said, " Life is ten percent of what happens to you and ninety percent of how you choose to react to it." When we see in us what God sees, we can speak like the psalmist, *"For You formed my inward parts; You covered me in my mother's womb. I will praise You for I am fearfully and wonderfully made. Marvelous are Your works, and that my soul knows very well." [Psalm 139:13-14]*

God's Word assures us that we have been made righteous and justified by the blood of Jesus Christ. Our new nature imputes to our DNA receptors that we have high self-esteem when we accept what Christ has done for us at Calvary. As a born-again believer, you can feel confident that you have the mind of Christ and that you can imitate His character and His nature.

Here are five reasons why your self-image should be defined in Christ and not in the world's description of who you should be:

1. We have been predestined and adopted as children of God by our Lord and Savior, Jesus Christ. We are accepted in the Beloved which means that through faith in Christ alone, we are forgiven; we have been made holy, and blameless. No matter what you have done in life, you can be forgiven just for the asking.

   Father God looks at us through Christ as if we had never sinned. You and I now have the same privileges as biological children although we were adopted by God. This unmerited favor of forgiveness has been granted to us by the grace of God. Salvation cannot be earned nor is there religious works or moral effort we can do to earn it.

> *"For by grace you have been saved through faith, and that not of yourselves; it is the gift of God, not of works lest anyone should boast."* [Ephesians 2:8-9]; *"But to all who believed Him and accepted Him, He gave the right to become the children of God."* [John 1:12]; *"For as many as are led by the Spirit of God are children of God, these are sons of God. For you did not receive the spirit of bondage again to fear, but you received the Spirit of adoption by whom we cry out, "Abba Father." "The Spirit Himself bears witness with our spirit that we are children of God."* [Romans 8:14-16]

This tells you and me that self-worth is a choice. Each individual has to decide to believe who God says he or she is or live with feelings of worthlessness and low self-esteem. Salvation gave you the right to claim your new identity in Christ. When trials come, don't return to bondage which is the old, negative way of thinking. Let the weak say I am strong, and the poor say I am rich because of what the Lord has done for me!

2. We have been redeemed from the burden of a sinful nature. To be redeemed means to be set free, to save from a state of sinfulness and its consequences, to restore honor or the reputation of, to receive ownership of by paying a specific sum. The payment in full for our restoration from sin cost Jesus everything. He paid a debt He did not owe because we owed a debt we could not pay. To those who may still be suffering from the guilt of having an abortion, prostitution, child abuse, neglect, fornication, or other crimes, once you receive(d) Christ as your Lord and savior, sin no

longer has power over you; the grace of God through faith in Christ has set you free.

"Christ has redeemed us from the curse of the law being made a curse for us: for it is written, cursed is everyone that hangs on a tree (cross). [Galatians 3:13]

"In whom we have redemption through His blood, the forgiveness of sins according to the riches of His grace." [Ephesians 1:7]

Christ was cursed for us that we might be set free to reclaim our position as sons of God. Grace does not give believers a permit to sin. You will become a slave to whom you decide to obey, whether of sin leading to death, or of obedience leading to slaves of righteousness and holiness to produce much fruit for the kingdom of God.

3. We have been given power to triumph over Satan. Jesus gave us authority to use His name to cast out demon spirits that come to torment the mind of believers. "Behold, I give you power to tread on serpents and scorpions, and over all the power of the enemy, and nothing shall by any means hurt you." [Luke 10:19] You have power over depression and oppression, as well as power over manipulating spirits, controlling spirits, principalities, and powers of darkness.

   The enemy looks for a portal, or entry gate to your thoughts. Satan is not omniscient in that he doesn't know your state of mind until you tell him things like, "I'm sick... my diabetes... I might lose my job or home... I can't go because I don't have any money, or I can't afford...." When you show a lack of faith, the enemy is right there to continue to feed you negative, self- defeating thoughts and mental images until you accept his way of thinking instead of what God says about your situation. Negative thoughts will cause a victim mentality. God said you are more than a conqueror! The name of Jesus is a strong tower of refuge and strength! God hears and honors words of faith, but Satan listens for words of defeat so that he can destroy your self-worth.

4. Jesus promised to send a Comforter, to teach, guide and help you. Jesus told the disciples that, *"If you love me, and you will obey what I command; and I will ask the Father, and He will give you another Comforter to be with you forever-The Spirit of Truth. {John 14:15-17]; "However when He, the Spirit of Truth comes, He will guide you into all truth. He will not speak on His own authority, but whatever He hears He will speak; and He will tell you what is yet to come. He will glorify me by taking what is mine and making it known to you." [John 16: 13-15]*

    The Holy Spirit is the third person of the Godhead. He is the "parakletos" the Greek word for helper. The Godhead works in perfect unity to fulfill God's plan for the present day and throughout eternity. No matter what it looks like, God is still in complete control of heaven and earth.

5. Jesus promises to be with us always. This short and powerful promise assures believers that God is our sufficiency for all our needs. He himself says,

> *"I will never leave you nor forsake you. The Lord is my helper; I will not fear. What can man do to me?"* [Hebrews 13:5-6] *He also comforts us with these words, "Because he has set his love on Me, therefore I will deliver him; I will set him on high, because he has known my name. He shall call upon Me, and I will answer him; I will be with him in trouble; I will deliver him and honor him. With long life I will satisfy him; and show him my salvation."* [Psalm 91:14-16]

Your self-image will never rise above your own confession of who you are no matter how many times you are told that you are valued and significant. You have to believe that you really are who God created you to be. You have to believe and receive what God has so freely given. It is disobedient and disrespectful to disregard God's principles while living in His presence.

Unbelief can impede progress in every area of your life including your marriage, your ministry, leadership ability, promotion on your job, and other opportunities in life. The Word of God brings balance, wholeness, and peace, instead of unrest, doubt, and fear. By knowing your Christian identity, you will have the confidence and boldness to be a more powerful witness for the kingdom.

Change must take place on the inside, in the heart, or it will not last very long. The following example describes what happens when the truth is not accepted or believed. A plastic surgeon by the name of Dr. Maxwell Malt wrote a best-selling book entitled *New Faces, New Futures*. The doctor's theme was predicated on the idea that amazing personality changes can take place when a person's face is changed. However, after many years, Dr. Malt began to learn that even after plastic surgery, people did not change the way they see themselves. People were made exceptionally beautiful, but they kept on thinking and acting the part of an "ugly duckling." They acquired new faces, but they kept on wearing the same old personalities. In fact, he said that they would insist that they looked the same even after drastic changes were made. Their families and friends hardly recognized them, but psychologically they had not changed. Bottom-line, unless change is made in one's heart, the person continues to act and feel the same.

Real change only comes through much practice and determination. I believe that many believers fail to grow into their new identity in Christ because they don't want to put forth the intense effort it takes to reach a deeper intimacy with Him. Additionally, they need to invite the Holy Spirit to reveal truth and interpret the deeper meaning of scripture. *"Beloved, I pray that you may prosper in all things and be in health, just as your soul prospers." [3rd John 1:2]* The soul speaks of one's mind, will, and emotions. Until you set your mind on gaining knowledge and spiritual understanding, you will not have the power to overcome your carnal, fleshly desires and worldly behaviors.

A low self-image is based on a system of negative mental pictures and feelings that you put together about yourself. For example, a student named Victor Seribriakoff was told by his teacher that he would never amount to anything. As a result of this insult, he dropped out of school and did odd jobs for the next seventeen years. When he was thirty-two years old, he applied for a new job which required him to take an IQ test. The test revealed that he was a genius. Victor changed his attitude and started acting like a genius. He went on to write many books, and he became a wealthy businessman. This speaks to the fact that it's what's in you that counts and not what happened to you. As a man thinketh, so is he!

God created you to identify with the qualities He gave you. Father God is the life source of your DNA. You were created healthy and strong, but sometimes you may have to defeat sickness, lack and insufficiency, fear, doubt, worry, and other ailment that the enemy uses to try to defeat what God has blessed. Some causes of a poor self-image include:

1. Negative experiences_ If you grew up with lots of criticism, rejection, and disapproval, your environment helped create a feeling of insecurity, inadequacy, and worthlessness.

2. Negative thinking_ Negative thinking patterns can corrupt every area of life. Negative thinking can reinforce feelings of inferiority, self-doubt and self criticism which can cause a mental rut that is extremely destructive to one's self and others around them.

3. Guilt_ Thoughts of poor self-worth can be caused by unresolved guilt because the sins of the past cannot be forgotten.

4. Life's disappointments_ Everyone grows up with dreams, goals, or expectations for the future. When one can't measure up, a failure syndrome may develop which increases feelings of uselessness, and inadequacy that can decrease one's self-confidence.

5. Social pressures_ Society imposes certain standards that can make one feel second-rate or under-appreciated, or even abnormal. Many people grow up in a society that slowly robs them of human dignity and self-worth.

As a child of the King of Kings and Lord of Lords, it's time for you to develop a desire to be the king, and lord that your DNA has predestined you to be. As a believer, this world is not your final destination; therefore, you don't have to accept an attitude of "less than" when you have a Father who is "more than" enough.

"Now unto Him who is able to do exceedingly abundantly above all we can ask or think according to the power that works in us." [Ephesians 3:20]

Negative thinking doesn't belong to the sons of God. Remember, your DNA has been changed from the earthly to the eternal. Your Father is more than abundant in everything you will ever need. He can do exceedingly abundantly above. He supplies you with more than you even know how to ask for or think you may need. The seeds of greatness for physical, emotional, and spiritual well-being were created in you at birth, but you have to choose to make them grow. When you know who you are, you will think and speak the truth. You will learn the value of self-acceptance. There will never be a person who is more important to God than you because He does not regard one person higher than another. God loves you for who you are, not for what you do.

To improve social interactions, see the list below for action steps that help build self-esteem and self-confidence:

1. Always greet people with a smile. Take the initiative to state your name first and always extend your hand first. Look the person in the eye when you speak.

2. Don't compare yourself to others. You are an original and unique. Don't become a cheap copy.

3. Make it a habit to listen to inspiring self-development programs that educate you.

4. Invest in your own knowledge. Enroll in professional development classes. Make reading self-help books including the Bible a habit.

5. Just say thank- you for a compliment. Neither play-down or play- up the value that is spoken to you.

6. Don't brag. People who show-case themselves or shout for service are actually calling for help.

7. Try not to tell others your problems unless they are directly involved with the solution.

8. Find successful "role models" that you can appreciate, and learn all you can about how he/she succeeded.

9. Select wise friendships. Associate with people who build your self-confidence.

10. Guard your tongue and your eyes. Don't criticize or condemn people. Remember, you are what you watch. Too often people exist on a diet of television, movies, and publications that is considered "junk food" which leads to malnutrition and poor emotional and spiritual health.

Your thoughts will influence feelings about yourself. Your attitude can make or break you, heal or hurt you, make friends or enemies, make you feel uptight or put you at ease, make you miserable or sad, and make you a failure or an achiever. Maintaining a positive attitude is a part of your spiritual DNA.

"What is man that You are mindful of him, and the son of man that You visit him? You have crowned him with glory and honor." [Psalm 8:3-5] You have been predestined for victory in your spirit, soul, and body. My hope is that you will choose to walk in your Divine calling.

And He said to me, "My grace is sufficient for you, for My strength is made perfect in weakness."

[II Corinthians 12:9]

Three

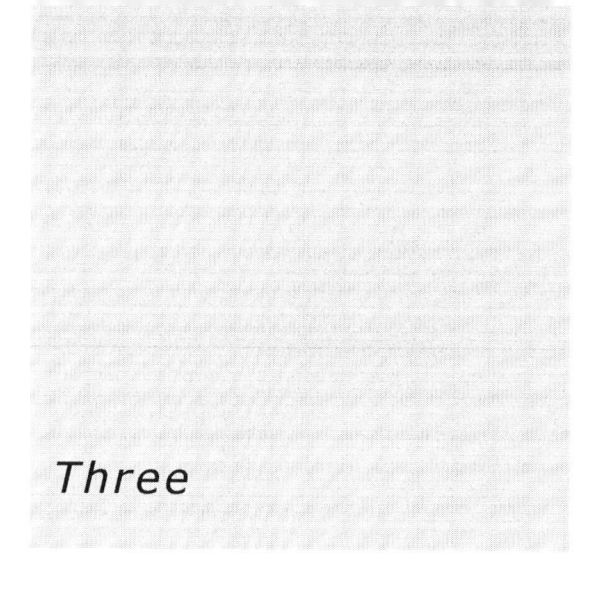

ABUNDANTLY BLESSED BY HIS GRACE

As children of God we are abundantly blessed by His Divine grace. One of the greatest aspects of God's love and compassion for His people is the principle of His grace which separates Christianity from other religions of the world. God transformed all humanity by inviting every man, woman, boy and girl in every nation of the entire universe to partake of His Salvation Plan by accepting HIS Divine influence of the heart. Grace in both Hebrew and Greek has the same definition of the word "charis" which means favor. Yet, many refuse the doctrine of grace through faith in Jesus Christ and His sacrificial death on the cross. Instead, they choose to live their lives in His presence, that is, in the world created by God, but people oppose His offer of salvation through faith in Jesus Christ. God will move heaven and earth to save sinners who cannot save themselves through their own effort.

Grace is defined as God's unearned, unmerited, and undeserved favor to vindicate sinful humanity. Grace is the first part of God's salvation process. A Christian is justified (past, present, and future sins paid for) by Christ's death as the Lamb of God. There is nothing that we as Christians can do to pay for our sins. *"For He made Him who knew no sin to be sin for us, that we might become the righteousness of God in Him." [2nd Corinthians 5:21]* God's grace shows us His favor and brings pleasure, gratification, and thanks to most believers. God gives His part such as forgiveness, eternal life and the power to live that life right now. Our part is to repent, surrender, and to reach out in faith for our own salvation.

When Jesus appeared, grace and truth appeared. The whole truth never came with the law that was brought to the people by Moses. *"For the law was given through Moses, but grace and truth came through Jesus Christ." [John 1:17]*

God's grace was exemplified on the cross of Calvary. The entire work of Christ in coming to earth, dying for sinners, and being crowned with glory is by the grace of God.

His sovereign act of drawing us to Himself is by His grace. *"But when it pleased God, who separated me from my mother's womb and called me through His grace, to reveal His Son in me, that I might preach Him among the Gentiles..." [Galatians 1:15-16]* Here, Apostle Paul describes God's desire for him to preach the gospel. Every element of salvation is the work of God through grace and not of our own making as men come to believe by the grace of God.

The terms "grace and salvation" have become almost synonymous. The principle of grace removed the death threat from us. Adam's fall brought spiritual death upon mankind. When Adam and Eve sinned by eating of the tree of the knowledge of good and evil, he affected himself and all of his physical seed that would come in future generations. *"For since by one man came death, by man also came the resurrection from the dead.*

For in Adam all die, even so in Christ all shall be made alive." [1st Corinthians 15:21-22]

God's saving grace makes provision for the salvation of all men. God delays judgment by giving men ample time to repent. Adam's disobedience produced spiritual death which caused the sin nature in man to produce the works of the flesh. As Adam's offspring, several things happened to us:

1. Adam's sin infected the human family and was passed down to every race and every generation.

2. All of the human race died spiritually (separated from God) and all of Adam's descendants were poisoned with the sin nature that caused spiritual death.

3. Human nature can only produce after its own kind; therefore, when it reproduces, it reproduces fallen, corrupt, and sinful humans. But by the grace of God, we believe we have been saved by grace through faith in our Lord Jesus Christ and not by our own works.

❖

Grace Versus Works

"Knowing that a man is not justified by the works of the law but by faith in Jesus Christ, even we have believed in Christ Jesus, that we might be justified by faith in Christ and not by the works of the law; for by the works of the law no flesh shall be justified." [Galatians 2:16]

"For as many as are of the work of the law are under the curse; for it is written."Cursed is everyone who does not continue in all things which are written in the book of the law, to do them. "For by grace you have been saved through faith, and that not of yourselves; it is the grace of God, not of works lest anyone should boast." [Ephesians 2:8-9]

Just as a lost man cannot obtain salvation through good works of his own, neither can a Christian maintain his salvation by doing good works. Salvation is obtained and maintained by grace alone. God's grace made us secure by the price Christ paid for the removal of our guilty conscience which gave us righteousness with God. Because of Jesus, we don't have atonement for our sins; we have the remission of our sins!

"For Christ has not entered the holy places made with hands, which are copies of the true, but into heaven itself, now to appear in the presence of God for us; not that He should offer Himself often, as the high priest enters the Most Holy Place every year with blood of another. He then would have had to suffer often since the foundation of the world; but now, once at the end of the ages, He has appeared to put away sin by the sacrifice of Himself." [Hebrews 9:24-26]

By God's grace, all of the curse from Adam (sin and the effects of sin) was placed on Jesus so that all of the blessings might come upon us. We are exceedingly, abundantly blessed in Christ. Jesus took our sin and gave us forgiveness; Jesus took our sickness and gave us health and healing; Jesus took our diseases and gave us wholeness and wellness; He took our poverty and gave us prosperity; He took our spiritual death and gave us eternal life; instead of living under a curse, we received Abraham's blessings. What a mighty God we serve!

Sanctifying Grace

Christians need God's sanctifying grace to be "set apart" which is the grace that works within the true believer. The Holy Spirit works to make changes that will bring growth, maturity, and progress toward becoming Christ- like. As Apostle Paul said, *"By the grace of God I am what I am, and His grace toward me did not prove vain; but I labored more abundantly than all of them, yet not I, but the grace of God which was with me."* [1st Corinthians 15:10]

Only God can give us the spiritual transplant needed to supernaturally change our nature. It is impossible for us to change our own nature without help from the Holy Spirit.

"The heart is deceitful above all things, and desperately wicked; Who can know it? [Jeremiah 17:9]

"For though you wash yourself with lye, and use much soap, yet your iniquity is marked before Me," says the Lord God. [Jeremiah 2:22]

"Can the Ethiopian change his skin or the leopard its spots? Then may you also do good who are accustomed to evil. [Jeremiah 13;23]

"Who can bring a clean thing out of an unclean? No one! [Job14:4]

True repentance is a complete change of heart, change of mind, and change of attitude which causes us to turn from sin; go in a new direction, and turn to God for help that will bring about a changed lifestyle. Before the Prodigal son could change, he had to come to himself. "But when he came to himself, he said, 'How many of my Father's hired servants have bread enough and to spare, and I perish with hunger! I will rise and go to my father, and will say to him, "Father, I have sinned before heaven and before you..." Father in these verses also represents Father God to whom we must show true repentance and make a lifestyle change to be saved.

The grace of God calls us to true repentance. Salvation means that Jesus is not only our savior, but we must make Him Lord by removing "self" from the equation as there can be only one of us in charge. When we totally surrender to Jesus, God's grace will allow the blessings that we don't deserve to increase. We can do nothing to earn salvation. By faith we receive this free gift from the Lord.

God gives us sanctifying grace that will cause several changes to become evident both within and without.

1. *"The Spirit Himself bears witness with our Spirit that we are children of God." [Romans 8:6]*

2. We have a new sensitivity toward sin, and we do not practice sin like we did before salvation. *"Whoever has been born of God, does not sin, for His seed remains in him; and cannot sin, because he has been born of God. In this the children of God and the children of the devil are manifest: Whoever does not practice righteousness is not of God, nor is he who does not love his brother." [1st John 3:9-10]*

3. We have a new attitude toward the world and its value system. *"Do not love the world or the things in the world. If anyone loves the world, the love of the Father is not in him. For all that is in the world_ the lust of the flesh, the lust of the eyes, and the pride of life_ is not of the Father but is of the world. And the world is passing away, and the lust of it, but he who does the will of God abides forever." [1st John 2:15]*

4. We love the Lord Jesus and will experience persecution or rejection at times for our Christian faith. *"For the grace of God that brings salvation has appeared to all men, teaching us that denying ungodliness and worldly lusts, we should live soberly, righteously, and godly in the present age..." [Titus 2:11-12]*

"If the world hates you, you know that it hated Me before it hated you. If you were of the world, the world would love its own. Yet because you are not of the world, but I chose you out of the world, therefore the world hates you." [John 15:18-20]

God's grace gives us Divine influence to minister in such a way as to manifest the life of Christ as members of His body. Serving allows the spiritual gifts to be in operation.

"But to each one of us grace was given according to the measure of Christ's gift. Therefore He says: "When He ascended on high, He led captivity captive and gave gifts to men ...And He Himself gave some to be apostles, some prophets, some evangelists, and some pastors and teachers for the equipping of the saints for the work of ministry, for the edifying of the body of Christ." [Ephesians 4:7-8; 11-12]

We have God's grace, "charis" which also means favor because we are made in His image. Every offspring looks like the father in some way. God favors us because we are made in His image. Once we have repented, and are baptized, we receive the Holy Spirit. We are now children of God. We have God's seed in us. Now we are growing in grace as the Holy Spirit continues to teach, guide, convict, and reveal to us the will of God.

Grace does not give anyone permission to sin. Some people think that God will just give a pat on the hand for sin and ignore it. God is a God of grace as well as a God who judges sin. Jesus' crucifixion was the fulfillment of the requirements for the law against sin. There is nothing else any of us can do to pay for sin. Jesus paid our sin debt in full on Calvary. You see, we owed a debt we couldn't pay; Jesus paid a debt He didn't owe!

❖

The Cost of our Grace

The world has caused some believers to minimize the gift of God's grace which brings favor and eternal life. Cheap grace is believing without obedience or intellectual assent without commitment. Cheap grace says you don't have to be serious about purity or righteousness. Cheap grace says that Jesus died for me, so I don't have to change. Cheap grace allows you to justify your behavior by focusing on the "things" of God more than God Himself. That is, cheap grace seeks what's in His hand and not what's in His heart.

Cheap grace is a license to sin which does not allow death to the flesh or to a self-centered lifestyle. There are those who continue to live a life of fornication, adultery, lying, bitterness, anger, unforgiveness, pornography, and the list goes on. *"What shall we say then? Are we to continue in sin that grace might increase? No, how shall we who died to sin continue to live in it?" [Romans 6:1-2]* Grace was and is not cheap. The gospel of Christ is the Gospel of the kingdom, which is the same Gospel of grace and the Gospel of truth as they are one in the same.

The grace appropriated to us for forgiveness of sin cost God everything. It cost the life of His Son, Jesus. God didn't allow the fallen angels to be redeemed by the blood of Jesus, but to God we are valuable and significant. He saw us as worthy of the sacrifice. When I see how some people choose to repay Him for saving them, I wonder if they really take time to know how loving and compassionate He is. He is my everything; for me to live is Christ!

Grace was not cheap to Jesus either. It cost Him his life. It is difficult to imagine what it was like to be spit upon, mocked, whipped with a cat of nine tails that pulled flesh from His bones, cursed at and denigrated. He took all this and died as a curse for humanity upon a cross for our sins. He became sin for us and suffered the wrath of God all alone. Grace is not cheap. Jesus lost his friends, pride, power, security, and connection to the Father. How can we dismiss our sins as if nothing happened? It cost Christ the most precious gift, His life, yet He said, "Father forgive them for they know not what they do." [Luke 23:34]

Cheap grace is not concerned with what Christ did for us, but what He can do for me as an individual. Sometimes the anger at God for not granting immediate gratification will cause some to blame God and leave the faith. He gave His life to let us know how much He loves us; therefore, patience and obedience to His Word are still paramount. Often a wish is delayed because the person can't handle it right now. God looks at everything from a kingdom perspective. If a desire distorts His plan for your life, there will be a time of withholding that thing until it will do the greatest good for you.

Cheap grace is not concerned with righteousness, but with duty and obligation. On the other hand, true grace is not about us; it is all about what God expects of me. True grace is not demanded, it can only be given to us through the power and person of the Holy Spirit. Speaking or praying with a strong conviction of faith is not a demand. Cheap grace is ritualistic in that the person only goes through the motion of praise, prayer, or worship without having an intimate relationship with the Holy Spirit. Sometimes acts of worship may be done to impress others, to seem "spiritual" when the heart is not engaged. God knows and judges the heart. *"For the Word of God is living and powerful, and sharper than any two-edged sword, piercing even to the division of soul and spirit, and of joints and marrow, and is a discerner of the thoughts and intents of the heart."* [Hebrews 4:12] No man can do anything to earn God's grace or approval. Only Christ is approved by God. Grace is the power of God in us to help us do the right thing. True grace is attained through faith in God, and this kind of grace is not cheap; it will always result in good works and bring honor to God when it is based on kingdom purpose.

❖

Grace that Empowers

Another aspect of God's grace is His divine power that gives us empowerment and enablement to do all things in Jesus' name. God's desire is for Christians to experience His power and ability that allows us to accomplish what we would not be able to in our own strength. You may have heard the song, "The Blood Will Never Lose Its Power." When Jesus was crucified on the cross and resurrected from the grave, He gained victory over Satan which put us back in righteousness or right standing with God. Let me state this another way; the Lord of all came to earth and faced death to rescue all people. We received His DNA again, and our spiritual receptors began to take on the image of Christ. The power of grace through faith is still available to draw all men to God. However, there are many who prefer to live in the presence of God without accepting the power and principle of His amazing grace.

God's Divine grace not only gives us faith for salvation, but His grace also gives us the on-going power to do the right thing. Grace through faith gives us the opportunity to do good works and avoid making poor choices knowingly as some believers do. As born again believers, we are empowered with spiritual guidance from the Holy Spirit to overcome temptations. Jesus was led into the wilderness by the Holy Spirit to be tempted by the devil. The Bible says He fasted forty days and forty nights, and He was very hungry. Two observations are noted here: 1) The enemy will usually tempt you when you are distressed or disadvantaged; and 2) You will not know true obedience to God until you have had the opportunity to disobey God. Jesus was tempted in his friendship, finances, and His faith. This time of testing showed that He was human, and that He really was the Son of God. He overcame Satan's temptations by relying on faith in the Father. He reminded Satan with the words "It is written" meaning that God's Word was His lifeline and nothing would make Him bow down to any worldly condition or fleshly desires. Christ triumphed over

Satan through His death on the cross which gave believers power to overcome sin. If you are repeating any sexual sins and immoral behaviors, let the examples of Christ help you defeat temptations in your life as well.

The nation of Israel was also led into the wilderness to teach them humility and total dependency on God. Due to their disobedience, an eleven day trip took forty years to complete. Satan constantly fights those who follow and obey God. If Satan never attacks you, it may be possible that the two of you are going in the same direction. Satan wanted to make Jesus declare His Kingdom prematurely. If Jesus had been disobedient, He would not have died on the cross, and we would not have the opportunity to receive eternal life. Jesus knew who He was and kept His focus on His calling and His connection to His father's DNA. He chose to delay immediate gratification for long term imminence as King and Lord of all.

Apostle Paul was empowered by a Damascus road experience that transformed him from a murderer to a Christian. God's grace of enablement changed his life and empowered him to preach the gospel to the Gentiles and to write most of the New Testament Epistles. Wherever there is a move of God, the Holy Spirit, grace, and faith will be present to bring about a total transformation. Allow your faith to reach out and declare in the supernatural all that God has promised to you. Grace will work on your behalf to appropriate what you could not do on your own. Paul was a murderer until God's grace changed him. Grace changed him from hurting others through hatred and bitterness. Grace enabled him to be transformed to be able to love God and his fellowman. God's Divine influence of grace enabled Paul to love those he once hated. God's grace allows us to produce much fruit when we operate in the grace principle which enables and empowers us to do good works .

The Holy Spirit empowers the church to operate in the spiritual gifts that edify the body. *"Now to each one the manifestation of the Spirit is given for the common good. To one is given through the Spirit, the Word of wisdom, to another the Word of knowledge by mean of the same Spirit, to another faith by the same Spirit, to another the gift of healing by the same Spirit, to another the workings of miracles, to another prophecy, to another discerning of spirits, to another different kinds of tongues, to another interpretation of tongues."* [1st Corinthians 12:8-10]

There are certain things we can do on our own accord; these are considered natural abilities and talents. But the grace of God empowers us by the Holy Spirit with specific gifts to serve others. If we tried to use these gifts in our own strength, we would fail. When you operate in the Spiritual gifts, you have to rely on the grace of God to show you His ways, and to give you His Words. When you share your faith, you have to rely on God to give you boldness and courage. You have to trust God to demonstrate His power within you; otherwise, you will fall flat on your face every time. God's Divine grace empowered by the Holy Spirit transcends our natural talents and abilities to enable us to do what we cannot do on our own.

God's Divine grace is His empowerment for every believer to have victory and success in this life. You are empowered to live a life that pleases God whether you do so or not. When you were born again, you received the ability to obey the Word of God. Your Spirit received a transfusion with divine DNA to enable you to surrender your will to God's will through the shed blood of Christ who sacrificed Himself for our eternal security. God's grace through faith gives us divine influence for supernatural results. The Bible tells me that I can do all things through Christ. This really means what I can't do in my own natural ability, I can do by the grace of God. God's grace frees you and me from trying to accomplish everything in our natural strength, but to rely on God to fulfill His principles and promises to us by faith.

The beauty of grace is that we receive strength in weakness. Apostle Paul prayed that God would heal his infirmity; instead, God spoke to him saying, *"My grace is sufficient for you, for my strength is made perfect in weakness. Most gladly, therefore will I glory in my infirmities, that the power of Christ may rest upon me."* [2ⁿ Corinthians 12:9] You have to receive this enabling power of Christ in order to overcome personal battles of sickness, distress, rejection, temptations and many other attacks that come to weaken your defense against the evil one. You will not always be victorious in your own strength. Don't give up like non-believers do when they can't solve a problem by using their own intellect. His grace is sufficient to help you overcome obstacles in life. Confess out loud that God's grace empowers me when I'm weak. You will be encouraged to find that your faith for grace will propel you to believe beyond what is happening right now. There have been many times in my life when I could not rely on natural results, but my total dependence was in His grace.

Christ gave us His ability to experience an abundant life as His followers. *"Most assuredly, I say to you, he who believes in Me, the works that I do he will do also; and greater works than these will he do, because I go to My Father." [John 14:12]* This grace of God is a free gift that was imparted to us the day we were born again; the moment we accepted Jesus Christ as our Lord and Savior. Jesus loves us so much that He gave us power to allow the Holy Spirit to work in us to enable believers to accomplish more than He did. Christ's earthly ministry lasted three years, but our earthly ministry should last throughout our lifetime to reach many more people if we are diligent and obedient.

Grace empowers us to serve God with peace and endurance. Grace enables the power of God to ignite the power receptors within us in such a way that makes all things possible to those who believe. When we work in our own strength, we suffer burn-out and fatigue. As co-laborers in Christ, we have more strength and endurance.

"Wherefore we receiving a kingdom which cannot be moved, let us have grace, whereby we may serve God acceptably with reverence and godly fear, for our God is a consuming fire." [Hebrews 12:28-29] Let us put our trust in Christ. Those who follow Christ are part of His kingdom, and they will withstand the shaking, sifting, and burning.

Whatever happens here, our future is built on a solid foundation that cannot be destroyed. God's grace ensures our confidence and enables us to overcome circumstances, situations and obstructions that threaten our peace from day to day. Remember, we have the enabling power of grace to endure all things through faith. Christ took all our sins on Himself on the cross at Calvary. Grace compels us to continue His ministry of reconciliation and restoration of those who need peace and endurance to live a victorious life on earth as it is in heaven.

The Gospel(good news) is a result of God's grace; Christians are called by grace, man is saved by grace, and we are justified by grace. Grace is God's kindness toward us when we don't deserve it. God grants grace to sinners in the pardoning of their sins, and bids them to accept eternal salvation through faith in the finished work of Christ. He even gives the measure of faith to receive salvation. Yet, there are those who refuse His grace through faith for salvation. However, they want every luxury and financial advantage this world has to offer. Many people want the provisions of God, but they defy living by the principles of God! Amen?

Your employer should not receive more respect than God. Employees will study the manual to learn the rules, attend workshops and training sessions to improve their skills in order to become more efficient, and they will even work overtime or weekends. It is more important to study to show yourself approved in the knowledge of Christ. If you desire the provisions of God, shouldn't you be readers and followers of His manual also?

Scripture does not teach universal salvation-for by grace you are saved through faith. Grace should not be abused, and we should not continue in sin to receive more grace. Man has a responsibility to live right, and grace helps man to understand that God desires to show him favor instead of condemnation. However, the Book of James reminds us that, *"Faith without works is dead." [James 2:19]*. Faith is our part of the equation which empowers us to do good works to show gratitude to God who loves us unconditionally. Scripture records, *"That as sin has reigned unto death, even so might grace reign through righteousness unto eternal life by Jesus Christ, our Lord." [Romans 5:21]*

God loves us so much that He designed a way to rescue humanity from total destruction before the foundation of the world. In other words, grace was created by God before it was needed. The law came by Moses, but truth and grace came by Jesus Christ who fulfilled all of the law since man was incapable of keeping the law due to his sinful nature. Grace is active even though many are passive about receiving what Christ provided with His shed blood on the cross. Sinful man could not settle the sin debt for Adam's disobedience in the garden; therefore, God gave His only Son as a ransom for us. God is longsuffering toward us, not willing that any should perish, but that all should come to repentance. [2nd Peter 3:9]

One day God's grace will no longer be available. This is why we compel the unsaved to receive salvation. *"But the Day of the Lord will come as a thief in the night, in which the heavens will pass away with a great noise, and the element will melt with fervent heat; and the works that are in it will be burned up." [2nd Peter 3:10]* Grace broke the power of sin over our lives; by grace we are fully justified and made righteous; by grace Jesus allowed us bold access to the throne of God which means we no longer have to live defeated lives. We have been redeemed by the blood of the lamb. What a mighty God we serve!

❖

Grace as God's Divine Favor

Divine favor is another attribute of God's grace. The Greek word for grace is "charis" which is translated as favor. Favor is part of our spiritual DNA. As believers in Christ, we have abundant favor from God. When you believe what God's Word says, you activate faith to pursue His promises until they manifest. The Bible says, *"For You O Lord, will bless the righteous. With favor You will surround him with a shield." [Psalm 5:12]*

If you are a born again child of God, this scripture is for you. You were made righteous, and the barrier that once existed because of sin has been destroyed by Jesus Christ who gave His life for us. Now we have right-standing with our heavenly Father which aligns us for supernatural favor. Favor means to win approval; favor also means to have divine advantage or special privilege, to be unusually loved, trusted, and provided for without any extra effort from you.

Divine Favor supersedes natural circumstances and situations as God's favor will override earthly conditions to bring unstoppable momentum for victory in every area of your life.

Favor is a concept of Divine prosperity. With Christ as our Savior and Lord, we are blessed with salvation and wholeness. The world defines prosperity as money, riches, wealth, social standing, and political influence. Godly prosperity refers to much more than money. God wants us to be made whole in every aspect of our lives.

Salvation is the most excellent gift, but we also have been blessed with a Divine advantage for the exceedingly abundant favor of God for increase spiritually, mentally, physically, relationally, and financially. Jesus Christ has redeemed us from the curse of poverty so that we may be blessed with Divine prosperity in all things. *"Beloved, I pray that you may prosper in all things and be in health, just as your soul prospers." [3rd John 2]*

The God kind of favor allows us to prosper in all areas of life. Grace is God's Divine favor to bless us spiritually so that we can be born again, Spirit filled, and daily living as Christ-ones.

- Mental prosperity gives us freedom from fear, anxiety, and depression in order to operate with a sound mind filled with God's peace.

- Physical prosperity means that our body is healed, healthy, and free from sickness, pain, and disease. Our relationships have Divine favor when we are living free from unforgiveness, anger, resentment, morbidity, and to have the blessings of God on our marriage and family.

- Financial favor comes as a result of giving our tithe and offering, blessing the poor, and all our bills are paid. God does not oppose Christians having money. The problem comes when we allow money and things to control us.

The Bible tells us that God is our source. The world's source for financial favor comes from depending on a job, business, people, the lottery, or the government. God gives us favor, wisdom, ideas, and the ability to create wealth. God's purpose for abundance is to promote the gospel so that Christ can be preached to all people on earth. *"And you shall remember the Lord your God, for it is He who gives you power to get wealth, that He may establish His covenant which He swore to your fathers, as it is this day."* [Deuteronomy 8:18]

I believe that some Christians are so influenced by the world's financial system that they can't wrap their mind around Kingdom principles of prosperity. Some believers fail to prosper financially because they have been subjected to erroneous teachings which include:

- Tithing is an Old Testament principle and not for today.

- Jesus was poor; therefore, we should identify with His poverty.

- God blesses His people spiritually, but not financially.

- God is pleased with whatever we give because He knows our heart.

So often we want the favor of God, but we are disobedient to the principles of God which cause us to live a life of compromise especially when it comes to finances. Believers can't serve two masters. Christianity is not a supermarket where you can pick up what you want and disregard what you don't like. We must receive and obey the whole counsel of God's Word [James 1:22]. Even though the Bible is very clear about kingdom finances, some believers still follow man-made traditions. They might say, for example:

- You can tithe whatever you want such as your time, your talents, or your office space.

- It's all right to use your tithe to help your neighbor.

- If you can't afford to tithe right now, God understands.

Sowing and reaping is God's plan for financial favor. When we give, whether tithes or offering, we sow something in God's Kingdom in faith that it will grow. Any money we invest into the

Gospel above the tithe is an offering. Just as a farmer reaps what he plants, we reap what we plant in God's Kingdom. We have legal claims and Divine favor as tithers:

- The windows of heaven will pour out blessings upon our finances, jobs, and businesses.

- We are protected from Satan, the thief and devourer.

- The source of our income is protected.

- Each time we give an offering, we have a 100-fold return on our financial investments.

- God will pay us back with interest, and we will not lack. [Malachi 3:10-11; Mark 10:29-30]

Do you think that God wants the world to be blessed and for you, the born-again believer, to live in poverty and lack? So often we need and want the favor of God, but we are disrespectful to the Word of God. Obedience to God and His Word pays. If you are giving to God out of a heart of love, and not out of a legalistic law, then God's favor and blessings are going to be upon your life.

Make no mistake about it; God is an extravagant God! He created the diamond mines in Africa, the gold and silver deposits in various parts of the world, oil in the Middle East, granite in caves of Brazil, and it was God who hung a diamond star as big as the earth in the sky. I think you get the picture. To quote a line from Bishop Bronner, "If you have a choice of being spiritual and poor or spiritual and rich, please choose spiritual and rich." God has no problem with your status as long as you seek His kingdom first. Living with lack and insufficiency doesn't impress God. Your success makes it look like you have a prosperous Father instead of a dead beat dad!

God's grace appropriates Divine favor and Divine assistance to the believer. God grants preferential treatment by providing advantages or a favorable position to those who act on His principles and promises. God showed favor to His people by liberating them from slavery.

"And the people took their dough before it leavened, their kneading troughs being bound up in their clothes upon their shoulders. And the children of Israel did according to the word of Moses; and they borrowed of the Egyptians jewels of silver, and jewels of gold, and raiment: And the Lord gave the people favor in the sight of the Egyptians, so that they lent unto them such things as required. And they spoiled the Egyptians." [Exodus 12:34-36]

God wants to take the wealth of the sinner and put it in the hands of His people. God's Word is the same yesterday, today, and forever, and neither you nor I can change it. God's people should possess the land today like they did back then. God's people should have the gold, the silver, the businesses, the houses and land by divine intervention, but when we compromise our faith, we compromise our position of favor.

I believe God wants to bless you with the same favor that He poured out on His people including Abraham, Isaac, and Jacob. We have their DNA, as well as God's covenant of grace and favor secured for us by the blood of Jesus. The word covenant in Hebrew means "cut" where blood flows, to make an incision. I believe God has a better way for you and me. It is based on God's gift of divine favor in these latter days. This favor is for everyone! I believe God wants to open new doors, provide supernatural appointments, and bring new ideas for business when you are ready to receive. Even before you see things turn around, I believe God is working on your behalf, and when He floods you with favor, it is going to be exceedingly, abundantly above all that you may ask or think according to the power that works in you. The same favor that works in the Bible is coming to you!

Christ's sacrificial death on the cross, His burial and resurrection gave us unmerited, unearned grace and favor that, in the natural, we do not deserve. God's favor was not only for Abraham, but for every born-again believer. He wants to make you a blessing so that you will be a blessing to everyone you meet. God's principles of grace and righteousness operate together. Righteousness is the life and nature of God that come into us when we are born-again. In other word, it's like joining a prestigious group or club. You are privileged to enjoy all the rights, rewards, security, and advantages of membership. As Christians, the difference is that faith in Jesus Christ is required, and you are no longer condemned, guilty, inferior, or forsaken because the blood of Jesus has made us righteous, and membership will last throughout eternity because of God's unmerited grace and favor.

Divine favor and grace operate through faith and love. We can see this kind of favor operating in the life of Daniel. He and all the Israelites were prisoners in Babylon. Daniel obtained so much favor with the leaders of the land that he was elevated to prestigious positions in the Babylonian kingdom. Even though the circumstances were stacked against him, Daniel eventually became the prime minister of Babylon.

Good things happened to Daniel because of God's favor. Even when he was thrown into the lion's den for praying during the time when prayer was forbidden by the king, Daniel came out without a hair singed or the smell of smoke on him. I believe the lions became supernaturally toothless and clawless when faced by God's Divine favor on Daniel. Daniel loved and trusted God to grant him favor. Daniel expected a victorious outcome. The book of Ephesians says there is special favor for those who sincerely love Jesus. *"Grace (favor) be with all them that love our Lord Jesus Christ in sincerity." [Ephesians 6:24]*

You can be just like Daniel. Call yourself a success and expect promotions to come your way. See yourself highly favored, with good things happening on your behalf. Confess your belief for the impossible and allow God's supernatural favor to work for you!

Queen Esther placed a demand on the favor of God in her prayers and petitions. In order to receive favor and answers to prayer, you must walk by faith. That means you are going to have to believe it and act on it before you see a request manifest in your life. If you are crying, complaining and worrying, you are not in faith. Worry cancels faith. It is interesting to see how Queen Esther put herself in the Lord's hand as she went into the king's chamber, and God gave her favor.

"Then said the king unto her, what wilt thou, Queen Esther? And what is thy request? It shall be given thee to the half of the kingdom.

And Esther answered; If it seems good unto the king, let the king and Haman come this day unto the banquet that I have prepared for him." [Esther 5:3-4] As the story of Esther goes, the king granted her request. Haman, who wanted to destroy the Jews, was hanged and the nation of Israel survived.

Additionally, I believe that Martin Luther King Jr. was favored by God to be America's "Moses" as he advocated nonviolent techniques of Gandhi to liberate African Americans and impoverished people everywhere. Dr. King inspired and informed America and the world of what an integrated and unified United States of America could be like if people were not judged by the color of their skin, but by the content of their character. When God wants to speak to a nation, He raises up a prophet to change the course of history. God is still in charge of His people.

"My sheep hear my voice, and I know them, and they follow Me. "And I give them eternal life, and they shall never perish; neither shall anyone snatch them out of My hand. " My Father, who has given them to Me, is greater than all; and no one is able to snatch them out of My Father's hand. " I and My Father are one."[John 10:27-29] Just like Moses, Dr. Martin Luther King Jr. became a leader of his people by the grace and mercy of God.

Throughout the Bible there are examples of God's favor. Favor brought Ruth, a Moabite, preferential treatment. As she gleaned from Boaz's field, she received supernatural increase. Boaz invited her to eat at his table, and she eventually married Boaz which gave her a place in the blood line of Jesus Christ. Abraham and Sarah birthed their son Isaac when she was ninety and he was one hundred years old.

Joseph became the second in command of Egypt in a time of famine. Joseph was successful even in a foreign land. His Egyptian master saw that the Lord was with him and made all he did to prosper in Joseph's hand. Therefore, he found favor and served as overseer of his master's house, and all he had, he put under Joseph's authority.

Even after Joseph was falsely accused and thrown in prison, he became a leader and interpreter of dreams by divine favor. Joseph was able to tell Pharaoh the meaning of his dreams, and God also gave Joseph divine wisdom to tell Pharaoh how to store grain that would sustain his kingdom for the seven years of famine. God's favor allowed Joseph to become ruler over all the land of Egypt. All surrounding countries came to Egypt to buy grain from Joseph including his brothers who had sold him into slavery.

These are only a few of the things favor will do for those who believe. You also have favor activated in your life because you are or can be born-again and called out of darkness into His marvelous kingdom. God wants you to prosper. God wants you to live in good health. God wants you to have a prosperous soul by believing in His Word, and living by His principles. We are not here just to occupy space, in His presence. We are here to take dominion and to evangelize the world until He comes. Amen?

"And do not be conformed to this world, but be transformed by the renewing of your mind, that you may prove what is that good and acceptable and perfect will of God."

[Romans 12: 2]

Four

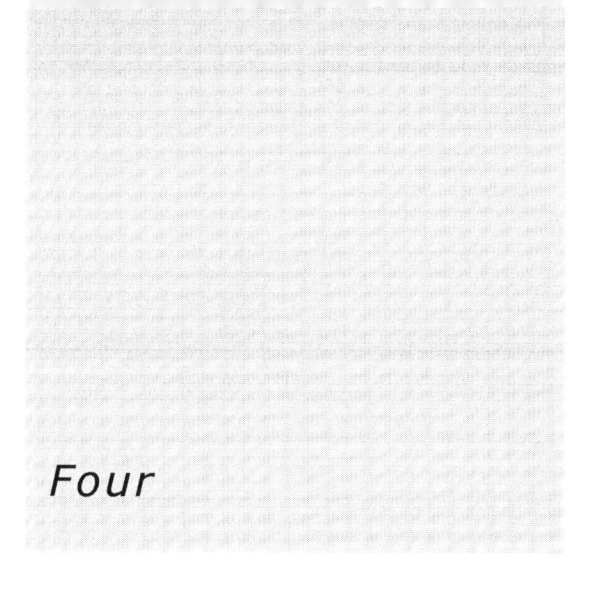

RENEWING THE MIND-A LIFESTYLE EXPERIENCE

As children of God, it is imperative that we renew our minds to function with God's truths, God's thoughts, God's ideas, and God's actions. Your mind has the power to determine the way you think about yourself and others, as well as how you conduct your entire life. Your actions will follow your thoughts. Remember, God put His DNA in Adam, but he was still deceived by Satan. We also have His DNA. Do you think you can overcome Satan without renewing your mind? If you don't learn to deal with negative thought patterns, you will never have what God planned for you. You will never be who He created you to be. If you refuse to change negative thinking, you will have the life you choose, not the life God wants you to live.

I have often wondered why so many Christians make little progress beyond being born again, although accepting Christ as Lord and savior is the greatest decision we will ever make. When I was younger, I thought that Christians automatically changed as they became older. Later, I realized that old age didn't change people, that going to church every Sunday, singing in the choir, quoting scriptures, nor speaking in tongues made them change either. This was a mystery to me as to how Christians could confess Christ as their Lord and savior, yet they could still sin like Satan. Then God gave me a new revelation about myself and other believers as to why Christians often think and act like unbelievers.

One generally accepted myth that believers must overcome is the idea that when we were converted or born again, our soul (mind, will, and emotions) was instantly renewed. Actually, our spirit was instantly transformed, and by the grace of God we were made righteous when we accepted Christ. However, our soul is in the process of changing day by day if we study and apply the Word of God to change behaviors that do not line up with godly principles.

The new birth changes your spirit, but renewing the mind changes the soul. You may think as I did that Christians have it all together, only to discover that some blood bought Christians, including us, continued to do the same things after salvation as we did before salvation, such as drinking, smoking, going to clubs, using profanity, committing adultery, living together before marriage, lying, being disrespectful to parents, irresponsible, out of control, abusive, manipulative, and the list continues. Whether these acts were done out of ignorance or intentionally, people will continue to be deceived if their minds remain un-renewed. The truth is that nothing changes for the better if it is left to improve on its own.

When Christians really wake-up and see the light, the church will experience a new revelation that will cause a worldwide revolution. Much teaching has increased an awareness of the battlefield of the mind; however, many believers we know are still confused, depressed, and miserable people who are not learning, growing, and maturing in their Christian experience. After reading the next few pages on renewing the mind, I hope you will make a conscious decision to live differently. I believe you will see clearly what the enemy is doing to keep believers in a state of emotional manipulation. Then I believe you will fight your way to victory. Every day you will be motivated to fight to take back your joy; fight to take back your peace; fight to take back the destiny that God planned for your life by giving the enemy no place! You have a right to every promise of God, but without renewing your mind to think about what you think about, like Adam, you will fall prey to fear and doubt which can allow mediocrity to minimize your ability to maximize your life's potential in Christ.

The spirit, soul, and body were created to maintain harmony and balance. I have a better understanding of why so many of us Christians fail to break away from Satan's grip and remain immature in Christian living. We think it is okay to live in His presence, to gain financially, and to attain what the world has to offer, yet we fail to respect His principles and His plan for our lives. The enemy seems to have our spiritual neurotransmitters tuned to a demonic frequency that leads to weapons of mass destruction instead of kingdom reconstruction. The problem lies in the soul where the mind is waiting to be repaired so that it can live in harmony with the DNA that's in the Spirit realm.

God wants to be involved in every aspect of our lives. The Bible reminds us, *"Now may the God of peace Himself sanctify you completely; and may your whole spirit, soul, and body be preserved blameless at the coming of our Lord Jesus Christ."* [*1st Thessalonians 5:23*]

It is our Christian responsibility to mature in our mind as we mature in our physical bodies. In order to have a healthy body, one must choose the right foods, drinks, and exercise to stay healthy. In other words, you have to invest in yourself to maintain optimum health. Likewise, you have to make a conscious effort to mature mentally and spiritually. Once we answer the altar call for salvation, the transformation of the soul should begin. Born again believers should not live most of their lives as bottle fed Christians. I call them CEM-Christians as they go to church on Christmas, Easter, and Mother's Day. The "new" you will be transformed day by day as you meditate on God's Word and apply it to life situations. The Greek word for transformed is metamorphoo from which comes the English word metamorphosis that signifies a complete and total change from one life form to another. For example, a caterpillar goes through a metamorphosis when it becomes a butterfly. If your life is the same today as it was last year, you need to be transformed. In fact, retraining, repositioning, and restructuring your thought life should become a part of every believer's lifestyle.

God created man as a triune being (three parts) with a spirit, soul, and body. Actually, man is a spirit made in God's image and likeness. *"For in Christ lives all the fullness of God in a human body. So you also are complete through your union with Christ, who is the head over every ruler and authority."* [Colossians 2:9-10] NLT

Our spirit is the part of us that is God conscious and relates directly to God. Man also has a soul and lives in a body. The soul of man is made up of the mind or intellect, the will, and emotions or feelings. Our body is the vehicle that gives us mobility in this physical world. The soul connects the body and the spirit. If the soul (mind, will, emotions) is not renewed to the things of God, man remains carnal minded and ruled by his five senses.

Our mind is the number one favorite place for the devil to attack us. Temptation always begins with a thought. The devil attacked Eve in the Garden of Eden with a thought. That's why we have to cast down thoughts and imaginations by bringing every thought into captivity to the obedience of Christ. Our mind is valuable. It equips us to know, remember, think, and understand things. Our mind determines and directs our thoughts and actions and controls our mental attitude. Satan's first target is the mind, but his goal is to turn your heart from God back to the flesh which means that you continue to do things and say things that oppose God.

Flesh means a way of thinking that is unchanged or unrestrained. Satan uses your five senses to keep you bound to the flesh in order to corrupt your mind. When your focus is only on what you see, feel, taste, smell, or hear, there is no room for the things of God. That is why your mind is the battlefield where your victory in life will be won or lost.

The mental images that you meditate on for long periods of time will become strongholds as you begin to believe them in your heart. Those negative images and thoughts may become larger than what God has revealed in your spirit. The devil wants you to lose faith in God's word and God's principles and give up. Satan wants you to believe that nobody cares, that your dreams will never materialize, that life is just too hard so that he can control your thoughts. The Bible says to cast your cares on Him for He cares for you. Also *"Walk in the Spirit and you will not fulfill the lust of the flesh."* [Galatians 5:16]

If you refuse to deal with the negative thoughts that oppose the will of God, you will miss the hope and the future God has for you. Your life will be unfulfilled, and you will merely live in this present world without power, without victory, and without joy or peace. The greatest challenge you have as a believer is to renew your mind so that your soul, spirit, and body will live in harmony with God. Before we can communicate with God, our mind has to be renewed.

"I beseech (urge) you therefore brethren, by the mercies of God that you present your bodies a living sacrifice, holy, acceptable, to God which is your reasonable service. And do not be conformed to this world, but be transformed by the renewing of your mind, that you may prove what is that good and acceptable and perfect will of God." [Romans 12:1-2]

Your success in life will be in direct proportion to your ability to control your thoughts, your words, and your actions. Your mind is the control center for intellect and knowledge. If the mind is allowed to run rampant and produce thoughts, words, and actions without restraint, Satan will rule your life and your relationships. He will decide what you can have, and what you can do. The Bible tells us to "fear not" 366 times, yet we still yield to fear and doubt.

Who will you choose to obey?

- Satan wants to invade your mind, but God says you have the mind of Christ.

- Satan wants to render you powerless, but God says you have the power to walk on the enemy's head; that no weapon formed against you shall prosper, and everything that rises up against you shall be destroyed because you are His inheritance.

- The enemy comes to steal, kill, and destroy, but God gives us life and life more abundantly!

❖

A RENEWED MIND

A renewed mind imitates the mind of Christ by acting on what the Father says. Jesus said that He does only what the Father tells Him, not what man's intellect or ability dictates. Evidence of a renewed mind is as follows: A renewed mind...

1. Meditates on God's Word regularly.

    Psalm 1:2-3 *"But his delight is in the law of the Lord, and in His law he meditates day and night. He shall be like a tree planted by the rivers of water, that brings forth its fruit in its season, whose leaf also shall not wither; and whatever he does shall prosper."*

2. Has a way of thinking that obeys the Holy Spirit, not the flesh.

    Romans 8:5-6 *"For those who live according to the flesh, set their minds on the things of the flesh, but those who live according to the Spirit, the things of the Spirit. For to be carnally minded is death, but to be spiritually minded is life and peace."*

3. Settled to do God's will, no matter what the cost.

   Joshua 24:15 *"Choose for yourselves this day whom you will serve, whether the gods which your fathers served that were on the other side of the River, or the gods of the Amorites, in whose land you dwell. But as for me and my house, we will serve the Lord."*

4. Resolve to be positive minded with no fear, worry or bad attitude.

   Isaiah 26:3 *"You will keep him in perfect peace, whose mind is stayed on You."*

5. Always ready to repent or change any thought or behavior at any time. Romans 12:2 *"And do not be conformed to this world, but be transformed by the renewing of your mind, that you may prove what is that good and acceptable and perfect will of God."*

6. Committed to a lifestyle free from unclean thoughts and deeds.

   Philippians 4:8 *"Finally, brethren, whatever things are true, whatever things are noble, whatever things are just, whatever things are pure, whatever things are lovely, whatever things are of good report, if there be any virtue and if there is anything praiseworthy, meditate on these things".*

   Romans 8:14 *"For as many as are led by the Spirit of God, these are the sons of God."*

Do you see why it is so important to see with your spirit more than with your natural ability? Your spirit has the ability to see the same way your eyes can see. When you are born again and give God free access to all the things in your life, you will be governed by the Spirit of God within you. Christ in you, the hope of Glory. The Bible says, *"But seek ye first the Kingdom of God, and his righteousness; and all these things shall be added unto you."* [Matthew 6:33] Everything you need is in the Kingdom. When trouble comes, you don't have to be moved if you live with a Kingdom mindset. Your job, your position, and your economic system are supplied by activating a Kingdom mindset.

❖

AN UNRENEWED MIND

A person with an unrenewed mind believes only in the flesh and what he or she can accomplish within one's own effort. Listed below are characteristics of an unrenewed mind which:

1. Finds fault; seeks to criticize and judges others.

2. Lacks knowledge of the Word of God.

3. Allows worry, doubts, fears and negative thinking to dominate.

4. Focuses on money, food, sex, power, and other fleshly desires more than the things of the Spirit.

5. Refuses to change and only seeks to prove one's own beliefs.

6. Seeks control through weak, indecisive, and undisciplined thoughts.

7. Operates by emotional feelings, and mental assent rather than truth.

8. Speaks with a prideful sprit ruled by ego, innuendo and vanity.

Satan loves people with an unrenewed mind. He knows that they depend on self effort more than the Word of God especially when circumstances become overwhelming. Consequently, Satan can influence their outcome with negative ideas such as fear of failure, fear of rejection, fear of poverty and lack to bring about their destruction. Once fear has taken its toll, the individual becomes angry, bitter, and resentful. Satan's ultimate plan is to make you blame God for all your troubles so that you will ultimately turn your back on the only one who can help you-God. Only the renewed mind can prove what is that good, acceptable, and perfect will of God. You can't do anything in the flesh that pleases God; therefore, you should seek His approval first to avoid painful consequences.

To be renewed in the mind means to allow the Holy Spirit to change your way of thinking:

"That ye put off concerning the former conversation the old man, which is corrupt according to the deceitful lusts; and be renewed in the spirit of your mind; and that you put on the new man, which after God is created in righteousness and true holiness. Wherefore putting away lying, speak every man truth with his neighbor: for we are members one of another. Be ye angry and sin not: let not the sun go down upon your wrath: neither give place to the devil....Let no corrupt communication proceed out of your mouth, but that which is good to the use of edifying, that it may minister grace unto the hearers. And grieve not the Holy

Spirit of God, whereby ye are sealed unto the day of redemption." [Ephesians 4:22-30]

God's intention is that we should have a sound mind. A sound mind is balanced, that is, it is disciplined, healthy, free from weakness, and filled with knowledge, wisdom and understanding. *"Therefore gird up the loins of your mind, be sober, and rest your hope fully upon the grace that is to be brought to you at the revelation of Jesus Christ."* [1 Peter 1:13] To gird up the loins means to control our mind and our thinking. You can choose the kind of thoughts you think. You can choose to control the kind of thoughts you allow your mind to feed on and entertain. Apostle Paul says we must guard and protect our minds by thinking about what is true, honest, just, pure, lovely and of a good report. The Bible also instructs us to bring into captivity every thought and make it subject to the Word of God.

Satan wants to keep us in bondage because of a lack of knowledge and understanding. As the god of this world's system, he wants to keep Christians mentally poor and ignorant of God's Word. When I talk to some Christians, I can't help but to notice that he has done a pretty good job of deception. They prefer the doctor's medicine rather than the medicine of the healing scriptures. They prefer poverty instead of prosperity. They rely on self effort more than faith. They live in His presence, but refuse to live by His principles. Satan does not mind how much you know. His job is to keep you from putting what you know into action. Your words please Satan when all you can discuss is your failures, pain, sickness and diseases, losses, hurts, rejection and other negative situations and circumstances.

It is time for Christians to renew or transform the way they think. Through our salvation in Christ which is the "new birth" our spirit is already transformed. Mission is accomplished for our spirit man, but we must also allow God to help us transform our soul which is our mind will, and emotions or feelings. God's Word enlightens our spirit and gives us wisdom and understanding. The Word of God trains, educates, disciplines, teaches, and instructs our minds to help us with spiritual growth.

There is a special anointing on the Word of God that gives new life as it is designed to bring about a change and freedom. *"And have put on the new man which is renewed in knowledge according to the image of Him who created him." [Colossians 3:10]* Mind renewal converts the soul so that you are not ruled by your wants and desires anymore; instead, you crave the lifestyle and the mind of Christ. You now choose to live in your higher soul better known as the Spirit realm.

"Beloved I pray that you may prosper in all things and be in health just as your soul prospers."

[3 John :2]

Five

UNDERSTANDING YOUR SOUL

You are a spiritual being who has a soul, and you live in a body. God interacts with the spirit of a man, not through his physical senses. It is the spiritual part of you that experiences fellowship with God. The only way you can find true peace, love, and joy is through the rebirth of the human spirit by accepting Jesus as your Lord and Savior. Just as a person cannot develop naturally without food and exercise, neither can a person develop spiritually without spiritual growth. Remember Jesus' reply to Nicodemus when he asked how a man can be born a second time and Jesus replied, *"I assure you, no one can enter the kingdom of God without being born of water and the Spirit. Humans can produce only human life, but the Holy Spirit gives birth to our spiritual life."* [John 3:5-6]

In order for the soul (mind, will, and emotions) to grow, it must have spiritual food which is the Word of God or knowledge; wisdom which is respect for the Word; and understanding which is to apply God's Word to everyday life situations. If a man does not eat and feed his body, he will starve to death; likewise, man cannot grow or develop in his soul if he is deprived of revelation from the Holy Spirit. There must be a balance in the inner man or the Christian cannot grow. Your life will not prosper until your soul prospers. *"Beloved, I pray that you may prosper in all things and be in health just as your soul prospers."* [3 John 1:2]

The key to John's prayer is that your soul has to prosper before you can be whole. In order for your marriage to prosper, your mind has to be renewed to understand a covenant relationship with your spouse. In order for your finances to prosper, your mind has to be transformed to understand Kingdom economics. In other words, you will prosper in direct proportion to your ability to be taught by the Spirit *and the Word.*

"Therefore, if any man be in Christ, he is a new creature; old things are passed away; behold, all things are become new." [II Corinthians 5:17] The Bible also says, *"It is written, man shall not live by bread alone, but by every word that proceed out of the mouth of God."[Matthew 4:4]*

Balance between mind, spirit, and body brings equilibrium and harmony to your life which gives you compassion for those around you. Your mind has to be renewed from day to day in order to be able to receive and act upon the plan of God for your life. Your soul or mind is a work in progress. Your conversion experience gave you the power to overcome carnal, lustful, selfish desires of the flesh. The question is will you listen to the old man, or will you readjust your thinking to live according to the principles and promises of God by exemplifying the life of Christ? The Gospel is not served buffet style where you can pick and choose only what you want on a given day. The Gospel is the "Good News" of God that will never change or lose its power.

Again, your soul is not the same as your spirit. If you can understand the difference between your soul and spirit, you would see why it is possible to be a born again Christian with a "new spirit," yet struggle with making the right choices due to an unrenewed, or unchanged soul. For example, Mr. Christian says he is converted, but he verbally and or physically abuses his wife or child behind closed doors. Mrs. Christian says she is saved, but she is intimately involved with someone other than her husband. Miss or Ms. Christian goes to church every Sunday and to Bible study on Wednesday night, but she allows her boyfriend to "sleepover" now and then. These behaviors are unacceptable as Christians. Until the mind is renewed to make people think about their actions and to change with the help of the Holy Spirit, they may live to be sixty or seventy years old without living in God's good, acceptable or perfect plan even though they claim to have been born again with His spiritual DNA.

"Even though our outward man is perishing, yet the inward man is being renewed day by day." [II Corinthians 4:16] In other words, the soul and spirit are renewed *as we walk with the Lord*, although the physical body is dying daily.

Part of Christian growth is getting to a place where we can follow our "born again spirit" instead of our flesh. When your spirit reminds you to pray before going to work, but your flesh tells you to sleep a while longer and pray later, your soul is the controller. I am reminded of a time when I personally faced this dilemma. I had to drive almost an hour to arrive at my school by seven a.m. My alarm rang at five a.m. so I had a good excuse to pray later, but the Holy Spirit told me to wake up and pray at four a.m. Reluctantly, I obeyed. To my amazement every morning there was a traumatic event at that school. One morning as I entered the parking lot, a teacher with diabetes fainted, and I was able to pray with her until she regained consciousness and transported to the hospital.

Another incident involved a student who lost consciousness in his classroom. The school secretary made an all points call asking me to assist him until the ambulance arrived. I found him prostrate on the floor, gasping for breath. I remember praying for him until help arrived. The ambulance driver asked me to continue praying in the ambulance until they connected him to life support equipment. About six weeks later, he returned to school, and I can't express the joy I felt as we hugged each other in the hallway that day. His teacher said he was doing fine. I remember consoling several co-workers who lost loved-ones unexpectedly. I was frequently asked to pray for individuals and their family members.

I began to see why I needed to pray each morning in order to have spiritual guidance and strength available to assist others in a time of need. By energizing my spirit each morning and submitting to God's plan, I was allowing my spirit to be the controller instead of my flesh. I'm sure you have also allowed your spirit man to overtake your murmuring and complaining flesh multiple times as well.

The flesh constantly desires worldly, carnal, negative things. The reason God is concerned with purifying and renewing your soul is to help you make better choices that are controlled by your spirit instead of your carnal mind. Undisciplined thoughts can greatly influence your feeling and emotions which can cause you to make impulsive or unwise decisions. A renewed or disciplined soul is one that hears and chooses to follow the Holy Spirit. When your spirit man is the controller, your soul will be prosperous. Below are eight ways the soul can be renewed and made prosperous through the Word of God and a sincere desire to change:

1. Have a hunger to learn how to change. [Matt. 5:6]

2. Develop a mind that meditates on God's Word and acts accordingly. [Psalms 1:1-3]

3. Have a disciplined mind that agrees with the Spirit. [Rom. 8:6]

4. Focus on Godly thoughts and attitudes. [Matt 6:33]

5. Confess your faults openly and honestly to God and ask Him to change you. [James 5:16]

6. Have a mindset that dwells on Kingdom thoughts approved by God. [Col 3:1-10]

7. Take control over feelings and emotions. [II Cor. 5:17]

8. Keep a pure, positive, happy attitude towards life. [Phil. 4:8]

Please take time to read and meditate on these scriptures. Also memorize the scriptures that speak to you. If we love Jesus, we will not only want to follow Him, but we will desire to be like Him.

The Bible says, *"Love has been perfected among us in this: that we may have boldness in the day of judgment because as He is, so are we in this world."* [I John 4:17] We can rely on God's presence in our lives to love us and to give us boldness to reach out to others without fear today or in the final Day of Judgment when we appear before the judgment seat of Christ to receive our rewards.

You will receive the level of health and prosperity in life according to your desire and ability to renew your mind. Your soul connects your spirit and body to bring the physical realm and the spiritual realm into relationship with God in order for you to live and function in the natural world. As you hear things in your born again spirit, you will also hear it in your soul. Sometimes you may say "something told me...," or you may feel like the Holy Spirit has just spoken to you personally. This is the process of the soul communicating with the spirit as they are conjoined. Since your thoughts direct your decisions, it is far better to think on things that will allow you to experience a Christ-centered life style as there is no evil or darkness in Him.

You will either prosper and live in health as your soul prospers, or you will struggle and live beneath your blessings, even as your soul suffers. You must decide! The Prophet Hosea said, *"My people are destroyed for lack of knowledge. Because you have rejected knowledge, I also will reject you from being priest for Me. Because you have forgotten the law of your God, I also will forget your children."* [Hosea 4:6] A Lack of knowledge holds Christians in a life of mediocrity. You have already been redeemed by the blood of Jesus, and you possess God's own DNA; why would you allow your lifestyle to be controlled by your soulish realm that is bound by feelings, emotions, and carnal desires?

Some theologians believe that the soul and spirit are exactly the same, but scripture defines the soul and spirit as different.

"Beloved, I pray that you may prosper in all things and be in health, just as your soul prospers. [3rd John 1:2] NKJV

God wants the entire individual to prosper. *"Now may the God of peace Himself sanctify you completely, and may your whole spirit, soul, and body be preserved blameless at the coming of our Lord Jesus Christ."* [I Thessalonians 5:23]

Paul is praying that we be preserved "completely" in every part of our being. Then he lists each part of the human person separately. This verse illustrates the uniqueness of the spirit and the soul. Your spirit was sanctified, or made pure, when you were born again. However, the soul is being sanctified as an ongoing process as we renew the old mindset in order to think and act according to the mind of Christ. Hopefully, you are beginning to understand that your soul has to be renewed continually. A Christian life change begins on the inside and flows outward. *"A good man out of the good treasure of his heart brings forth good things, and an evil man out of the evil treasure brings forth evil things." [Matthew 12:35]* When your soul prospers, it brings forth much fruit, but a poor soul is full of negative thoughts, attitudes, and beliefs that are not based on Scripture.

❖

Soul Transformation

God designed us to prosper and be in health; therefore, poverty and sickness are not His will. We must accept God's Word as the highest and final authority. God's Word is higher than religious traditions, family and cultural beliefs, false teachings, and a selfish desire to believe only what your mind receives as truth. God's has exalted His Word even above His name. Heaven and earth will pass away, but the Word of God will stand forever. The Word of God tells us that if we want to reprogram our way of thinking according to His thoughts, we must renew our mind to understand and believe His Word. This is the great exchange. We give Him our low life and get his high life. We give him our death and get His redemption. We give Him our sickness and get His healing. We give Him our poverty and get His prosperity. As we let go of personal struggles in the natural realm, we receive what is His in the supernatural realm. What a mighty God we serve!

Soul transformations means, *"Whoever finds his life will lose it, and whoever loses his life on My account will find it."* [Matthew 10:39] It is evident that most people choose to hang on to what they have or believe even though that thing or belief does not give them the lifestyle they desire. For example:

The poor person hates poverty, but he/she will not change the belief system or lifestyle that keeps him/her in lack.

The overweight person hates the fat but won't do what it takes to get fit.

The alcoholic, or drug abuser hates the behavior but won't give up the habit.

The lazy person hates the feeling of dissatisfaction with life but won't give up his couch to make something happen.
By transforming your soul (mind, will, emotions), you can break every chain that binds you. With God's help you can stretch

yourself to increase your mental net worth so that your problems won't be repeated again and again.

Steps to transform the soul include:

1. Take responsibility for yourself and your life.

Don't blame God or other people for the condition of your life. Take full responsibility or nothing will change. If you don't make a paradigm shift, you will be sentenced to a life of mediocrity, just surviving instead of thriving.

2. Rethink what you believe.

What you assume to be right compared to what God says about the matter are two different things. Rethink those beliefs you learned while growing up. If you don't begin to rethink some of your beliefs, you will continue to live and make decisions based on thinking that is totally wrong. For instance, of the twelve spies only Joshua and Caleb survived. The other ten spies told lies and did not believe that God could help them take the land from the Canaanites. As a result, they were made to wander in the desert forty years. Are you wandering in a desert? If so, it's time to rethink what you think.

3. Reject your old ways.

This is one of the most difficult steps because old habits are difficult to break. The question is how bad do you want it? Until you want to change, and you decide to practice steps to change, you will not change the old way of thinking or acting. The Holy Spirit will help you take thoughts captive if you ask Him for help. When a deceptive thought comes to mind, reject it by saying, No! I don't want to think like this anymore, and I won't receive it. This breaks the cycle before it becomes an action.

4. Review your new way of thinking.

Practice thinking these new thoughts. Meditate on the Word while driving your car instead of listening to the radio. For example, if you have trouble with financial prosperity, think, I enjoy being debt free. It feels good to pay cash for things rather than charging them on a credit card. It's nice to have money in the bank or to purchase what I want without thinking about how much it costs every time I buy something. I have extra money to invest in my future. I have an overflow of money to invest in others. I control my finances! Your new way of thinking will help you become disciplined with money until you can become debt free.

The way you think about money makes a world of difference. It's not a matter of waiting for something big to happen outside of you; it is a matter of changing something inside of you. Remember, *"You will prosper and be in health, even as your soul prospers."* [3rd John 2] You have to believe that what God says is truth, or your soul (mind, will emotions) will never change. The Bible has 250 verses on money alone, yet there are those who prefer to live with a poverty spirit.

The Bible says, *"Do not worry then saying , 'What will we eat?' or 'What will we wear for clothing?' "For the Gentiles eagerly seek all these things; for your heavenly Father knows that you need all these things. "But seek first His kingdom and His righteousness, and all these things will be added to you."* [Matthew 6:31-33]

5. Restate your thoughts out loud.

The fact is, it is our mental net worth that controls what comes out of us. One's thoughts, beliefs, and attitudes will control life. There was a time when I spoke out my fears and doubts. What I said began to happen. I said things like "I don't have enough money" or "Money slips through my fingers" or "I think I have a bad cold." Guess what, those negative situations and circumstances manifested until I learned to speak positive words and scriptures over my life.

The 23 Psalm of David, he said that God prepared a table for him in the presence of his enemies, and that his cup runs over. Obviously, his needs and many desires were met. Believe that you receive all that you have need of, and my God shall supply all your needs according to His riches in glory by Christ Jesus. Hallelujah! Speaking thoughts out loud will lock them permanently in your mind, and positive results will follow.

❖

Results of a Transformed Soul

There are many benefits that you will experience when your soul is transformed.

- God will give you peace if your mind has been renewed and stayed on Him. Praying for peace is one way to have it, but being transformed by the renewing of the mind brings perfect peace that passes all understanding. The twins called fear and doubt will no longer be relevant. Like Jesus, you will be able to sleep through the storm. [Isaiah 26:3]

- You will live in right relationship with God without condemnation. A "religious" spirit helps the devil make sure Christians stay condemned. A transformed soul enjoys right standing with God and freedom from guilt. [Romans 8:1]

- You will live in holiness. Holiness does not come from any outward appearance such as wearing a certain style or color of clothes, or not wearing make-up. True holiness comes only when the spirit of the mind is renewed by daily living in the reality of God's Word. [Ephesians 4:23-24]

- You will walk in divine health. Divine health is for those whose minds have been transformed and renewed. Doctors say that more than eighty percent of all illnesses begin in the mind. Unforgiveness causes most autoimmune illnesses. Controlling your thoughts and having a victorious mind-set instead of a victim mind-set will provide wholeness and longevity. [3rd John 2]

- You will experience financial prosperity, favor, and increase. Some believers are poor because of the way they think. "He who sows sparingly, will reap sparingly, and he who sows bountifully will also reap bountifully. So let each one give as he purposes in his heart, not grudgingly or of necessity; for God loves a cheerful giver. And God is able to make all grace abound toward you, that you, always having all sufficiency in all things may have an abundance for every good work." [2nd Corinthians 9:6-8]

- Only Christians whose minds have been transformed will benefit from giving tithes and offerings. Giving bountifully means giving even above the tithe or ten percent of the gross income. When believers begin to think in line with God's Word, they will be in line for blessings multiplied back to them. When your soul is transformed, the Holy Spirit will give you wisdom to prosper without measure. "You will prosper and be in health as your soul prospers." [3rd John 2]

- You will stay teachable, always hungry for more of God's truth. You will not be stubborn or think you know everything. There is still room to grow in grace and in the knowledge of the Lord. Christians attend church every Sunday, but many refuse to hear or receive anything new from the Holy Spirit. We should stay hungry with great expectations for a new move of God every day. The early church operated in multiple miracles. It is unlikely that some churches today have ever witnessed a miracle. [Psalm 25:9]

- You will project confidence and boldness. Confidence will rise up in you because you are learning to believe in your God-given abilities that increase your strength and self-worth. Confidence is not arrogance, and boldness is not always loudness. You have decided that the rocks are not going to cry out in your place any longer because you know who you are in Christ. [Philippians 4:13]

- You will be diligent and disciplined. Discipline is a virtue. When you are strict with your spirit, soul, and body, the whole man will be under the control of the Holy Spirit.

- *"But I discipline my body and bring it under subjection, lest, when I have preached to others, I myself should become disqualified. "* [1 Corinthians 9:27] Discipline is a commitment to do what you say or to keep your word. It also means being committed to Christian principles without returning to works of the flesh.

The habitual thoughts of your mind control how you live. As a man thinks in his heart, so is he. Jesus commands us to do more than just believe in God; we are commanded to love Him with all our soul. *"You shall love the Lord your God with all your heart, with all your soul, and with all your mind."* [Matthew 22:37] The spirit and soul make up the heart of man. The word "heart" here, is not referring to the organ that pumps blood through the body; instead, it is used to describe a particular inborn temperament of the inner person. Scripture says, *"Even though our outward man is perishing, yet the inward man is being renewed day by day."* [2nd Corinthians 4:16] The inward man that is being renewed is the soul. We know the human spirit is reborn when a Christian makes Jesus the Lord of his life.

The inner struggle is the battlefield of the mind where you have to make a choice between following the flesh or the spirit. The word flesh refers to a carnal, worldly mindset, and not the body itself. The flesh is constantly desiring things that make it look good or feel good, but the born again spirit is joined to the Lord, and desires only godly things. The soul hears the argument between both sides and can choose to obey either the spirit or the flesh. For example, when your spirit tells you to pray, but your flesh says watch television, the weak Christian will follow the flesh, but the strong Christian will be led by the spirit. Your mind and your spirit were both created by God, but you must decide which one you will choose to set the standard for your life.

The reason God is so concerned with the renewal of the soul is that without it, you and I will be constantly controlled by our fleshly desires. In order to have the life that God gave us through the death of His Son, we must rely on His truth instead of how we feel about the situation. As mature Christians, our emotions ought to be sufficiently stabilized and disciplined to follow the Spirit.

"Blessed be the God and Father of our Lord Jesus Christ, who has blessed us with every spiritual blessing in heavenly places in Christ."

[Ephesians 1:3]

Six

REBORN TO REIGN IN CHRIST

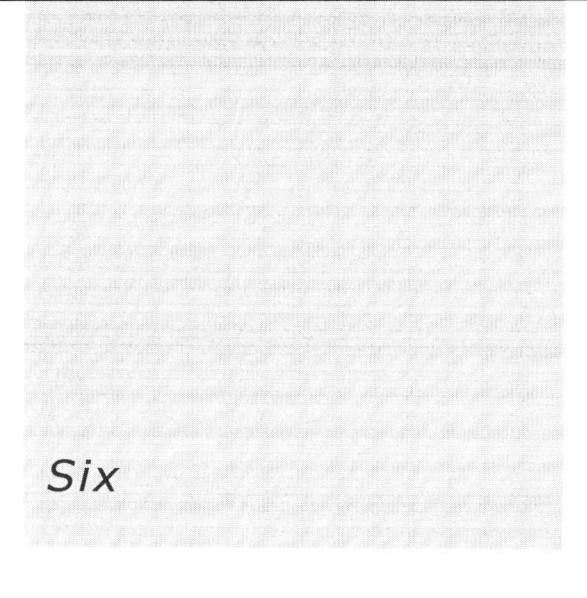

Salvation grants us the right to reign with Christ, but renewing the mind gives us the ability to accept our rightful position. It's time for believers to know that you are more than conquerors in Christ. It's time to come out of your little Christian closet and accept who you are, whose you are, and operate in the rights and privileges you possess. You were created superior to everything else on the planet, yet many believers are discouraged, depressed, defeated, or in denial about their true identity. When you look at the cup, is it half full, half empty, or completely empty? Do not believe Satan's lies! Let the following Biblical principles help you re-establish your true authority as a Christian believer.

❖

Reborn in God's Image

First, you have been reborn in the image of God. God took back your fallen nature and likeness from Satan and placed you in the "God Class." He intended for mankind to take rulership over all creation; therefore, He made man to be an exact replica of Himself. You are a spirit being that is able to communicate spirit to Spirit with God. Although you live in a physical body, the real "you" are spirit. Then God "blessed" him which means He created man to be fruitful, successful, and prosperous. God also gave you power and authority to take dominion on this earth, and the ability to live an abundant and joyful life. When true believers refuse to step up, then non-believers will assume leadership. The world system today resembles the days after the fall of Adam instead of the zoe, resurrected life that God intended.

At one time, Adam walked in supernatural power, revelation knowledge, and a high level of intelligence. God gave him power and dominion over the entire earth. He told Adam to "subdue the earth" which means to conquer it, master it, and to bring everything into subjection. Basically, he was told to keep everything in order. However, Adam's disobedience caused him to fall from his position of authority and dominion resulting in spiritual death. I detect that same spiritual death in the world today as believers continue to refuse to acknowledge that they are in the "God Class" which means to rise up and reign in Christ.

Adam placed himself under slavery and bondage to Satan, and sank to a level of defeat, failure, and mediocrity whereby he could no longer reign over the earthly kingdom entrusted to him by God. His blood line became diluted to the point that his DNA no longer had a resemblance to God. This same pitfall will happen to you and me if we refuse to rise up and oppose the ungodly practices of our day. Unfortunately, Satan still rules some of Adam's children as he did when he legally took control over the world system by taking authority and dominion from Adam.

Satan wants to corrupt your life like he did Adam. He wants you to live in a world consumed by materialism, lust, immorality, crime, addictions, self will and disobedience rather than conform to the principles of God.

Adam was living in the presence of God who supplied everything he needed, yet he allowed sin and disobedience to bring on spiritual death which made him a prisoner of Satan. He lost God's nature and produced children after the fallen image.

"And Adam lived one hundred and thirty years, and begot a son in his own likeness, after his image, and named him Seth." [Genesis 5:3]

Reborn with Christ- Likeness

Second, thanks be to God, that we have been reborn in the image and likeness of Christ to reign in this earthly kingdom. We don't have to live like the first Adam. Jesus came to earth to annihilate the devil and to regain everything he stole from Adam in the fallen world.

"Having disarmed principalities and powers, He made a public spectacle of them, triumphing over them in it." [Colossians 2:15]

"For this purpose the Son of God was manifested, that He might destroy the works of the devil." [1John 3:8] The blood of Jesus redeemed fallen humanity and reclaimed everything the devil stole from us.

The first Adam reproduced a fallen seed, but Jesus, the last Adam reproduced a new family after His kind, after His likeness and image.

"The first man was of the earth, made of dust; the second Man is the Lord from heaven. As was the man of dust, so are those who are made of dust; and as is the heavenly Man, so also are those who are heavenly. And as we have been born in the image of the man of dust, we shall bear the image of the heavenly Man." [1st Corinthians 15:47-49]

Anyone who is void of a new life in Christ is still under Satan's rule as he is the god of all unsaved people. The man who is not born again has a corrupt nature. The born again believer has the divine nature of God. When you are born again, you defeat Satan, and you get back the image of God. The Bible says that if anyone be in Christ, he is a new creation because old things have passed away; behold, all things have become new. This might be the time to ask yourself if you have been born again. If not, repent, that is, turn from a sinful nature and put on Christ. You can make heaven your home today by praying this prayer in faith:

Dear God in heaven, I come to you believing that Jesus died on the cross for my sins. I invite Jesus into my heart to be my personal Lord and Savior. Jesus, I ask You to forgive me for all my sins and cleanse me from all unrighteousness. Give me wisdom and knowledge to be able to live a Christian life. Teach me God's Word and baptize me with the Holy Spirit. I thank you, Lord, for saving me through your shed blood on the cross, and that I am on my way to heaven in the name of Jesus. Thank You God for eternal security in Christ Amen!

Because of Christ's obedience, we have favor with God! *"But thanks be to God, who gives us the victory through our Lord Jesus*

Christ."[1st Corinthians 15:57] Listed below are eight blessings we have because of Jesus:

1. WE have been accepted in the Beloved. Ephesians 1:6

2. WE have an inheritance that will never be lost. 1st Peter 1:3-5

3. WE have a hope and a future that can never be disappointed. Jeremiah 29:11

4. WE have a grace that can never be withdrawn. Ephesians 2:8-9

5. WE have a righteousness that can never be tarnished. 2nd Corinthians 5:21

6. WE have a peace that can never be disturbed. Romans 5:1

7. WE have a deliverance that can never be reversed. Romans 10:11-12

8. WE have a joy that will never be diminished. Psalm 16:11

❖

Reborn with Advantages and Privileges

Third, we have been reborn to reign in Christ with advantages and privileges that belong to every believer through the finished work of Christ on the cross. When Jesus said, "It is finished," He was not referring to His death alone. He was also speaking of the completion of all things that the Kingdom of God would grant to every believer.

For instance:

- Your lack and insufficiencies were finished.

- Your health and healing needs were finished.

- Your feelings of fear and doubt due to a sin conscious nature were finished. God's grace is greater than our sin.

- Your failures and unsuccessful attempts in life were finished. Because you belong to God, you get to try again and again until you win without condemnation from God.

All things are finished in Christ. He doesn't have to invent a solution to your problem because the answer is already available. However, God has many more new experiences in this life for us every day that we have not lived yet. When you are ready to receive the answers He has for you, He will allow His power to operate in you to receive all that you need. His Word says, *"Now unto Him that is able to do exceeding abundantly above all that we ask or think, according to the power that works in you...." [Ephesians 3:20]* This means that when you want to act on the Word spoken to you, God is here to empower you to exceed even above what you previously thought you could do.

You will begin to operate with supernatural favor, and those around you will see a new move of God in your life. You don't have to ask for favor when the anointing begins to operate. I remember attending a revival and as I was leaving, the man of God said that the Holy Spirit told him to ask me to minister the next two nights at his church. I usually minister in churches filled with friends and family, but I could sense that the Lord was doing a new thing. Both nights were powerful as the Holy Spirit moved upon that excited group of people.

When we finally recognize that our destiny is finished in Christ, we will stop waiting for some strange mystical thing to move us forward. Our spiritual transmitters will connect us with our Father's DNA to remind us that we have the right to paralyze Satan and all rulers of darkness. The way to take control of your destiny is to know who you are in Christ. Then you will learn to walk in confidence, and you will:

- Believe that you are who God says you are.

- Hear with supernatural ears and see with supernatural discernment.

- Receive what Christ has done for you through His finished work on the cross.

- Understand that God chose to love you unconditionally because He is good. You can't earn God's love by your works.

You have also been reborn to "put on Christ." At your first birth, you received your parents' characteristics, but when you were born again, you received a spiritual rebirth with the characteristics and likeness of Christ. You have been given the ability to imitate the life of Christ. You were born again as the incorruptible seed of God's Word. The seed of God was planted in your spirit to reproduce a divine birth and the Divine nature of Christ with an exact duplication of the "God Class." You now possess the characteristics, attributes, and abilities of Christ! Scripture tells us that, *"Having been born again, not of corruptible seed but incorruptible, through the Word of God which lives and abides forever."* [1st Peter 1:23]

It is amazing how much we can change when we put on Christ-likeness and ability! A great example of rebirth is seen in the life of Apostle Paul. He was first named Saul of Tarsus and known as one who persecuted Christians under the authority of the king. He hunted them down as criminals to kill them or put them in jail for heresy.

Saul was known as a merciless persecutor of the church which gave him favor with the king and non-believers of that day. Little did he know that one day on the Damascus Road, he would have an encounter with Christ Himself. Saul was blinded and led to a street called Straight where Ananias had been instructed by Jesus to pray for Saul to recover his sight. Later, he became a Christian who was baptized with the Holy Spirit, and his name was changed to Paul. Apostle Paul became the most determined to fulfill his call than all the apostles. He preached the Gospel of Christ and spent most of his life in persecution and hardship for the sake of spreading the Gospel throughout the known world of his time. He wrote two-thirds of the New Testament, and several of the epistles were written in a Roman jail where he was later put to death. What an awesome transformation from sinner to saint!

The moment you were born again, you received Christ's Divine nature as His finished work on the cross. Salvation, which is the born again experience, takes place in your spirit through the Holy Spirit. By your confession of faith, you are supernaturally transformed into the image of Christ. To be born again means to "put on" Christ which gives you the ability to:

- Experience a spiritual rebirth,

- Receive the nature, likeness, and ability of Christ,

- To be born again with the Spirit of God in you,

- To live and take dominion in the earth as sons of God!

"But as many as received Him, to them He gave the right to become children of God, to those who believe in His name: who were born, not of blood, nor of the will of the flesh, nor of the will of man, but of God." [John 1:12-13]

"Therefore if anyone is in Christ, he is a new creature, old things have passed away; behold, all things are new." [2nd Corinthians 5:17]

To be a "new creature" means you have passed from Satan's kingdom into God's Kingdom- a birth out of death into a new birth of life.

Your rebirth gave you the ability to "put on" the mind of Christ. *"Let this mind be in you, which was also in Christ Jesus: who, being in the form of God, thought it not robbery to be equal with God." [2nd Philippians 2:5-6]* What does it mean to have the mind of Christ?

1. The mind of Christ involves wisdom from God, once hidden but now revealed.

2. The mind of Christ is given to believers by revelation through the Spirit of God.

3. The mind of Christ gives believers discernment in spiritual matters.

4. The Holy Spirit indwells in us to enlighten us.

5. The mind of Christ means we share Jesus' perspective of love, humility, and obedience.

As ministers, all believers should have the mind of Christ which means we understand God's salvation and restoration plan for the world. *"The Spirit of the Lord God is upon me; because he hath anointed me to preach good tidings unto the meek; he hath sent me to bind up the brokenhearted. To proclaim liberty to the captives, and the opening of the prison to them that are bound; To proclaim the acceptable year of the Lord, and the day of vengeance of our God; to comfort all that mourn..." [Isaiah 61:1-2] KJV*

There are many benefits to having the mind of Christ in whom all the treasures of wisdom and knowledge are hidden. To have the mind of Christ means we must think as He thinks. We can still have the mind of Christ in a dysfunctional, carnal environment if we imitate Christ. We must decide to think good thoughts, whatsoever is true, honest, just, pure, lovely and of a good report.

Discern what is true about the situation, not based on feelings and emotions. Align your thoughts with God's Word. Learn to replace Satan's lies with God's truth. Ask God to reveal the lies you are allowing to control you and your relationships so that you can have better outcomes in life. Develop a spiritual relationship with Christ. Scripture tells us that if we are in Christ, we are heirs to the promises of God. It is in Christ that we live, we move, and we have our being.

When your mind and actions are filled with the character and nature of Christ, you will make choices that please God. It will be unthinkable to say you have the mind of Christ and still harbor resentment, bitterness, anger, unforgiveness, jealousy and envy toward others. As we meditate on the life of Christ, we gain insight through revelation from the Holy Spirit. He will teach us how to live according to Biblical principles as we read, study and seek His Divine guidance.

❖

Reborn to Reign as Kings

Next, we have been reborn to reign as kings. As children of God, we have been given authority to subdue, take dominion, and rule over the earthly kingdom. We have a God-given mandate to control situations and circumstances that confront us. We can reign as kings over powers and principalities of evil when we speak God's Word in faith. We need to stop living as cowards and exercise supernatural power over unnatural conditions as a normal way of living. Jesus tells us to speak to the mountain as he did during His reign on earth. He spoke to the mountain of sickness, blindness, deafness, hunger, demons, and death to mention a few, and He also proclaimed that we shall do greater things than these.

The mountain of death still reigns over the lives of unsaved people since they are under Satan's control. The lost have no enduring control over chaotic storms of life. We were once in bondage under the authority of Satan's rule; however, faith in Jesus Christ has translated us into the Kingdom of light where we have eternal freedom. Every believer has authority to be a lamp and a light to witness to unbelievers.

What does it mean to reign as kings? To reign as kings means that believers are obligated to proclaim the good news of the Gospel to the world. We are now joint heirs in partnership with Christ who has given us authority and dominion to win the earthly kingdom for Christ. Two-thousand years ago, Jesus gave a very clear mandate to the church. He specified that we are to preach and teach the Gospel to the world:

"Therefore go and make disciples of all nations, baptizing them in the name of the Father, and the son, and the Holy Spirit, and teaching them to obey everything I have commanded you. And surely I am with you always, to the very end of the age." [Matthew 28:19-20]

"Go into the world and preach the good news to all creation." [Mark 16:15]

"And this gospel of the kingdom will be preached in the whole world as a testimony to all nations, and then the end will come." [Matthew 24:14]

Jesus is the doorway into the Kingdom of God. Jesus said, "I am the way, the truth, and the life: no man cometh unto the Father, but by me." [John 14:6] A door is a portal through which we go from one place to another. Jesus is the door through which we pass from death into life, from fear to faith, from shame to righteousness, from guilt to pardon and from defeat to victory. This is a description of a contrast between the world's kingdom and the Kingdom of God.

Once we have entered into the Kingdom, we have to move beyond the doorway into a whole new world of riches and glory that lie within. Jesus said, *"I am the door: by me if any man enter in, he shall be saved, and shall go in and out, and find pasture….and I am come that they might have life and that they might have it more abundantly."* [John 10: 9-10]

Jesus is the head shepherd who brings us into the abundant pastures of our Father's Kingdom, and He wants us to participate fully in the joys, blessings, and benefits of His Kingdom, but He will not violate our will. Too often we only want to graze in a small corner of His abundantly vast, green pastures, but He will not violate our will. God will invite, inspire, and engage us, but He will not force us without our consent.

The degree to which we are willing to enjoy our Kingdom citizenship depends on the degree of our desire to be bold and claim what rightfully belongs to us through the blood bought price that Jesus paid for us on the cross, and what He has restored to us through His resurrection. To further illustrate Kingdom blessings and favor once we are admitted can be noted in the story of a traveler on a transatlantic voyage. There was a ship making her maiden voyage that a traveler desired to take. He only had enough money to pay for the ticket and nothing else. He stayed in his cabin and ate his peanut butter crackers and drank water while all the other travelers enjoyed the ship's festivities including a lavish captain's buffet every night.

The story goes on to say that on the last day of the voyage, the captain saw this man and asked him where he had been. The man replied that he ate in his room because he could not afford the meals that were served in the dining room of the ship. The captain responded by telling him that when he bought his ticket, everything else on the ship was free, compliments of the captain.

Unfortunately, too many Christians are stuck in the closet with an unwillingness to experience the fullness of the Kingdom that our Father has prepared for us. Just like the man on the ship, many believers leave their inheritance for thieves and robbers to steal because they refuse to think, speak, or act in faith. They are snared by the words they speak. *"Death and life are in the power of the tongue: and they that love it shall eat the fruit thereof."* [Proverbs 18:21]

In order to fulfill all that the Lord desires for us, we have to avail ourselves to all the Kingdom has to offer us. Only then can we begin to operate in the full potential God placed inside us. How can we teach unbelievers the whole Kingdom if we are unwilling to receive the whole truth? Will they be taught poverty or prosperity, healing or sickness, defeat or success, fear or faith, death or life? Yes, Jesus is the door to salvation, but we have been invited inside to experience His abundance, not just the bare minimum that life can offer. The life that He gives us is a life of fullness of His Kingdom, a Kingdom that has everything we could ever need or want that is filled with an inexhaustible supply. Kingdom living does not submit to defeat. Kingdom living moves forward with confidence, advancing in wisdom, power, and boldness that belong to us as children of God.

Reborn with All Spiritual Blessings

Reborn to reign as king also means that we have been blessed with all spiritual blessings of the Kingdom. God has given you and me supernatural authority, power, and ability to reign as kings and priests over His earthly kingdom. Authority means that you have been delegated power. One example of authority is that of a policeman putting up his hand to stop all traffic. The officer in himself does not have the power to stop all those vehicles, but the badge gives him authority to do so. Our natural ability cannot produce power in the spiritual realm. It is the authority or indwelling power from God that produces victory in the spiritual realm to set you free from all bondages.

The power to reign over the earthly kingdom is demonstrated in the Word of God. Authority is released by faith-filled words. When you as a believer begin to use the authority of God's Word to defeat the devil, several things can happen.

- You will command your circumstances to change.

- You will command drug dealers to leave your neighborhood.

- You will command sickness to leave your body.

- You will command cancer to throw itself in the dumpster because it is foreign matter that does not belong to you.

- You will accept your position as the conqueror that God intended you to be.

Be eager to use the authority that has been delegated to you as a believer. Remember what Jesus said, *"Behold I have given you the authority to tread on snakes and scorpions, and over ALL the power of the enemy, and nothing shall by any means hurt you."* [Luke 10:19] This is a prime example of what I mean by living in the presence of God. However, you will deny His principles and promise when you refuse to use faith-filled words. Spiritual authority has been imparted to every born again child of God, yet some believers will ignore the right to rule and reign over the devil; instead, they will let him trample heavily upon them and their family.

Authority is released by acting on faith-filled words when they are released. The centurion spoke faith-filled words when he said, *"Lord, I am not worthy that you should come under my roof: but only speak a word, and my servant shall be healed. For I also am a man under authority, having soldiers under me: And I say to this one; 'Go' and he goes; and to another 'Come' and he comes; and to my servant, 'Do thus,' and he does it." When Jesus heard it, He marveled, and said to those who followed, "Assuredly, I say to you, I have not found such great faith, not even in Israel!"* [Matthew 8:8-13]

The centurion stepped out in faith within his natural ability. He believed that Jesus had supernatural ability to heal his dying servant, and his servant was healed. The centurion stepped out in faith even though he was a Roman soldier. He believed in Christ's authority as a healer, and he wasn't even born again. How much more should we release the supernatural power of God by speaking faith- filled words of authority to our dead situations and circumstances.

I suggest three reasons that hold us back from taking authority over the enemy and walking in authority.

1. Some Christians don't know the Bible because they don't read it.

2. Some Christians read the Bible, but they don't believe what God's Word says.

3. Some Christians read the Bible, and they believe what it says, but they remain disobedient by refusing to practice or act on godly principles. They choose to live in His presence as part of the earthly kingdom without His power.

The born-again saints of God have unstoppable power and authority if they choose to release it. Jesus said, *"And I will give you the keys of the Kingdom of heaven, and whatever you loose on earth shall be loosed in heaven."* [Matthew 16:19] Wow! You have the power to release a blessing and stop a curse when you take your rightful authority in Christ. Religious thinking has brainwashed Christians into believing that they have to beg God to do something when all they have to do is to speak the Word in faith and allow God's Word to manifest.

We have been reborn to reign with every spiritual blessing that gives us dominion and possessions in Christ.

- We have every spiritual blessing including godly happiness, joy, Divine favor, and eternal life. [Ephesians 1:3]

- We have inherited the kingdom. As Abraham's seed, we are heirs according to the promise. [Galatians 3:29]

- We have access to the Father. [Ephesians 2:18] Sin had built a wall between man and God. A priest had to be the people's mediator in the days before Christ. Now we have direct access to the Father.

- We have all our needs met. [Philippians 4:18-20]

- We have the Holy Spirit. [John 16:13] Christ said that He would send another Comforter who will fill us with power and boldness, guide and intercede in prayer for us, seal us in Christ, impart gifts to us, show us God's love for us and reveal all truth to us.

- We have been made the righteousness of God. [Romans 5:1] *"Therefore having been justified by faith, we have peace with God through our Lord Jesus Christ."*

- *" For He made Him who knew no sin to be sin for us that we might become the righteousness of God in Him."* [2nd Corinthians 5:21]

- We have the love of God. [John13:34-35]. The main distinction that set believers apart from the world is the love of God. This unconditional, agape love replaces the law system of the Old Testament. Satan cannot by any means imitate God's love for us.

- We have salvation from sin and God's presence is with us.

"Neither is there salvation in any other: For there is no other name under heaven given among men whereby we must be saved." [Acts 4:12]

Emmanuel means God with us. Jesus said, *"And, lo, I am with you always even unto the end of the world."* [Matthew 28:20]

- We have authority to cast out devils in the name of Jesus and to heal the sick. [Mark 16: 17-18]

- We can rejoice that our names are written in heaven. [Luke 10:20] "Nevertheless do not rejoice in this, that spirits are subject to you, but rather rejoice because your names are written in heaven."

Since you have been blessed with all spiritual blessings of the Kingdom, let this be your daily confession:

> I will love others like I have never been hurt.
> I always have a positive attitude.
> I will not be overcome with fear.
> I am able to do whatever I have to do.
> I am strong, confident, and always encouraged.
> I submit my will to God's will promptly.
> I am very generous.
> I am very careful about what I say.
> I choose to enjoy my life every day.
> I think about what I can do to bless others.
> I choose to forgive others quickly.

As children of God, we have the capacity to walk in supernatural wisdom. We can ask God for the strength and ability to solve problems and to understand how to manage difficult situations. The devil has no access to our reborn spirit. The power of God in our lives looses, sets free, and breaks the power of sin imposed by Satan. Even though we live in chaotic conditions in the world, we have complete access to God's supernatural power to remove heavy burdens and destroy every yoke.

God wants us to graduate from the place of being affected by what's in front of us. God wants us to submit to the Holy Spirit so that we can make right choices and not be moved by our feelings, thoughts, and emotions. God intends for your will to yield to the Spirit. Eve in the garden relied on the soulish realm to be wise in her own thinking, but she was deceived. God said the day you eat of the tree of the knowledge of good and evil, you will surely die. Adam's spirit died and he became a flesh man. They were driven from the place of communing with God in the spirit to a place of trying to be wise in their own eyes. They wanted God's presence without His principles.

"Now faith is the substance of things hoped for, the evidence of things not seen."

[Hebrews 11:1]

Seven

LIVING IN KINGDOM FAITH

To live a life of faith, we have to know God's Word, to believe God's Word, and act according to God's Word, and not what our flesh or natural senses dictate to us. Faith is probably one of the greatest challenges because it means believing in something you cannot see. In the natural, we have two eyes and two ears that we received at birth. When we were born-again we received spiritual eyes and ears. As we grow spiritually, we begin to see with spiritual eyes and to hear with spiritual ears. By faith we can see the invisible!

What God reveals in the unseen realm has more reality than what we observe in the seen realm. For example, your faith for salvation comes from God, and it serves as the foundation for your faith walk. You believe that heaven is real although you haven't been there if you are reading this. The same should be true for all of God's promises such as healing, prosperity, promotion on your job, believing for the right husband or wife, and other promises you have from God. When you believe according to God's Word, find the Scripture(s) for that promise and watch God move according to your faith.

Faith That Unlocks Heaven

What is faith and how do we obtain it? Faith is the supernatural ability to believe in God without doubting His Word in order to make the impossible possible. Faith is grasping the unrealities of hope and bringing them into the realm of reality. Faith is living in the supernatural realm, naturally.

"Now faith is the substance of things hoped for, the evidence of things not seen." [Hebrews 11:1]

- **Now** faith is the substance of things hoped for, the evidence of things not seen.

- **Now** faith makes us certain of things we do not see.

- **Now** faith is the title deed for the things we hope to possess.

- **Now** faith requires us to be convinced that what we believe is true.

- **Now** faith believes before it sees.

Faith is the hand that receives what we need from God. Everything Jesus purchased for us on the cross of Calvary can be obtained by faith. In the New Covenant, the Holy Spirit allows believers to see beyond things in the natural, and look into the eternal when we choose to see through spiritual eyes. What we see becomes reality by faith which enables us to announce what already exists in

God's Word, thereby, causing the request to manifest in the temporal or seen realm. Faith is the bridge between the eternal and the temporal. To pray in faith is not just saying words, but intently waiting on God until we see by the Spirit what He is seeing.

God never promised to lead us by our physical or mental abilities. However, without the Holy Spirit, we depend on our natural eyes, ears, and other senses to dictate to us and record it as reality. What we see in the eyes of the Spirit is usually in direct contrast to what the natural eyes are reporting as fact. When we pray in faith through spiritual eyes, prayer is effective because we are praying in the perfect will of God. What God speaks brings things from the unseen realm into reality. The exciting thing about hearing God is that the Holy Spirit will enable believers to be "caught up" into the eternal realm to see the unseen. Once God reveals what exists from His perspective, we can acknowledge what God wants to perform in the natural world.

When Elijah stood before Ahab, he declared, *"As the Lord God of Israel lives, before whom I stand, there shall not be dew nor rain these years, but according to my word." [1st Kings 17:1]* Elijah proclaimed that it would not rain at his own word, not God's word because Elijah had crossed the realm of faith from the temporal into the eternal, and having seen the mind of God, he could declare what God showed him in reality. Elijah could speak with authority to King Ahab because he had already seen what would happen in the eternal realm. You can also speak with authority when you stop depending only on what you see in your natural environment. The Holy Spirit will teach you to speak words of faith that reach into the throne room of Heaven to receive the promises of God just like Elijah.

In order to pray a prayer of real faith, the mind has to come under subjection to the Holy Spirit. Three and a half years later, Elijah went to the top of Mt. Carmel, bowed down, and put his head between his knees and prayed that God would send rain again. Elijah kept his mind subjected in that position while he commanded his servant to check for results. And he said to his servant, *"Go up now, look toward the sea. And he went up, and looked, and said 'there is nothing.' And he said, Go again seven times."* *[1ˢᵗ Kings 18:43]* Elijah prayed unwavering until his servant saw a cloud the size of a man's hand. The rain came as God had revealed to Elijah.

Faith is seeing what is going on in the heavenly realm and declaring it a reality. Noah also peered into the unseen realm and watched God reveal future events. Then he came back to the temporal or (seen) realm and built an ark on dry land in response to the heavenly reality. At some point, I believe all believers have seen what God promised in the eternal and believed He would produce it in the natural. It may not be the Ark of Noah or the rain of Elijah, but you believed and received the petition you requested in faith. What is hindering you from acting on your answer?

My mother taught me how to stand in faith. I stated earlier how she peered into the eternal with her faith and believed that I would attend college even though my parents could not afford it. I will have you to know that is precisely what happened. God showed her exactly what she should do. According to her faith, I was to return to college and ask the dean of students to reactivate my loan which had been terminated due to insufficient funds for upper classmen that year. I asked her what I should say, and she said the Holy Spirit would tell me. I couldn't believe that my quiet, timid mother could speak so boldly about what God told her the previous night. I complied with her wishes and returned to campus the following day.

The dean asked me why he should go against the rules to restore my loan when he could not do so for other returning sophomores. I told him because it was God's will for me to continue my education. I even quoted from Alexander Pope's poem, "A little learning is a dangerous thing; Drink deep, or taste not the Pierian Spring." I guess he thought maybe I had learned something my freshman year after all. He pulled my application from beneath the stack and looked at it as if he were in a daze.

I couldn't believe what happened next. He wrote out a memo for me to present to the administrative department which would not only re-enroll me, but also pay my entire college expenses for the next three years. I lived on my mother's faith until I learned to be my own person by increasing my level of faith. I believe that God can do the impossible when we believe beyond what is temporal and reach out in the supernatural realm by faith to receive what God reveals in His promises to His children. My weak faith grew that day to a new level of strong faith that I would need so desperately in the years to come.

❖

Unshakable Faith

Hearing and believing what God said makes faith steadfast, immoveable, and unshakable. Faith is a spiritual force that grows, and develops in our lives. It comes by hearing the Word of God; however, it is our responsibility to cause our faith to grow by stretching our faith to operate at a higher level. A major opposition to avoid in order to have steadfast faith is listening to unbelief, doubts, and fears, that are opposites of faith. Unbelief comes by hearing the excuses of men. Doubt comes by hearing the voices of religious tradition rather than the true Word of God. Fear comes by listening to the lies of the devil. Doubt dilutes God's best for us when we decide He isn't moving fast enough, so we want to help Him bring it to pass.

Real faith is steadfast, immoveable, and unshakable!

Real faith is more than hope. Faith is now; hope looks to the future.

Real faith stands firm on what God's Word says until it manifests.

"For verily I say unto you, that whosoever shall say to this mountain, be thou removed, and be thou cast into the sea; and shall not doubt in his heart, but shall believe that those things which he saith shall come to pass; he shall have whatsoever he saith." [Mark 11:23] KJV Real faith stands firm when your symptoms say you are sick, real faith says you are healed, when your finances say you don't have it, real faith says you will receive it, when your doctor says it is over, real faith says you shall recover. Head faith or hope receives first; real faith believes then receives.

If God said it, you have it now even though you can't see it now. Abraham was strong in faith while Thomas was doubtful. Abraham's faith was steadfast, immovable, and unshakable. Abraham staggered not at the promise of God, but he was strong in faith giving God the glory. Abraham considered not his own body being old, but rather considered God's Word. Abraham was credited as righteous because he believed. [Romans 4:17-21] On the other hand, Thomas said he would not believe until he had seen Jesus and thrust his hand in Jesus' side and could see the holes in his hands and feet. [John 20:24-29]

Unshakable faith sees in the realm of the Spirit whereas carnal faith believes in the physical senses without the help of God's discipline or guidance. Head faith allows people to accomplish tasks through human effort. People respond to situations and circumstances based on how they feel at the moment with no regard for God's Word.

Seven attributes that describe real faith are as follows:

1. The God kind of faith is produced in the heart and released or spoken with your mouth. [Mark 11:23-24]

2. Faith is believing what God has said in His Word. [Hebrews 4:2; 2nd Corinthians 4:16, 18]

3. It is impossible to please God without faith. [Hebrews 11:6]

4. The Word of God is called the word of faith, and faith comes by hearing and hearing by the Word of God. [Romans 10:8, 17]

5. God has given to every Christian the measure of the God kind of faith. [Romans 12:3; Ephesians 2:8]

6. Jesus is the source, author, developer, and finisher of our faith. [Hebrews 12:2]

7. Faith is measurable and it can grow. [2nd Thessalonians 1:3; Acts 6:7- 8]

Gideon had to come out of his comfort zone to grow in faith. He learned to believe in God's word instead of relying on his feelings and family traditions. He grew from very little faith to the overcoming king of faith. His story from the Book of [Judges :6-7] is recaptured here:

God gave the Israelites the Promised Land, but they did evil in the sight of the Lord and forgot their God. God allowed the Midianites to rule Israel for seven years. When the Israelites planted their crops, the Midianite band of thieves would come and raid their fields at harvest time leaving the Israelites with nothing to eat. They took their livestock, sheep, goats, cattle, donkeys and striped their fields bare. The Israelites cried out to God for help. Gideon was threshing his wheat at the bottom of a wine press when the angel of the Lord appeared and said, "Mighty man of God, the Lord is with you." "Go and rescue Israel, The Lord is with you..." Gideon fleeced the Lord to get approval for his victory by praying for dew one day and dryness the next. After this test, he gathered 32,000 men to go to battle against the Medianites, but 22,000 went home timid and afraid. With 10,000 men left, God told him to keep only the men who were watchful and drank water from their hands. Now, Gideon had to fight the Medianites with only 300 men so that everyone would know that God won the battle!

Gideon divided the men into 3 groups, each with a ram's horn and a clay jar with a torch in it. After surrounding the Medianite's camp, they were instructed to blow the horns and break the pictures at the same time. God caused the Medianite army to fight against each other with swords. Those who were not killed fled in panic. Gideon chased them until he triumphed over them. The people wanted Gideon to be their king, but he said God is Israel's king. However, he served Israel as a Judge and ruled over Israel for many years.

Like Gideon, in order for faith to grow, you have to stop listening to what you think is right and see through the eyes of faith. You have to be willing to abandon old ways, unproductive thinking, and avoid some relationships which may include family members in order to have the unshakable kind of faith. Gideon was a man of little faith. His self pity, insecurity, and fears, made him doubt what the angel of the Lord had said. He also fleeced God and challenged what God said to him, *"I will be with you always."* Gideon felt deserted and began to ask these questions: *"If the Lord is with us, why is this evil on us? Where are the wondrous works of our Father? The Lord has forsaken us and given us the Medianites."*

Even though God had spoken victory, Gideon refused to operate in faith. Gideon persisted in weak faith by making excuses even when he was called a mighty man of valor or bravery. He was filled with self pity and responded with a victim mentality when he said:

- My family is the poorest in my clan. (Manessa)

- And I am the least in my father's house.

- O' Lord, I can't deliver Israel.

Many people struggle with these same self-defeating issues today, even though we have Christ, our kinsman redeemer, who sacrificed His life for us. The devil wants to render you dysfunctional like he tried to defeat Gideon. Maybe you are living with abuse, rejection, feelings of inferiority, unemployed, uneducated, or maybe you are quite wealthy, but lacking in family support, or feeling unloved, but I am here to tell you that you are a mighty man or woman of valor! And I know for a fact that God is with you no matter what it looks like!

Gideon stretched his weak faith from hiding in a wine press to thresh wheat to keep his family from starving, to great faith. He became the leader of the army that saved his country, and ruler of the nation of Israel. God is not a respecter of persons which means He doesn't care who you are. God can still use you, and He doesn't care if you are rich or poor, who your relatives are, if you are the president, a genius, whether you own a porsche or a camel. He loves you, but you have to love yourself enough to want to change. It is your unshakable faith that moves Heaven, not pity. My mother taught me to stretch my faith no matter what it looks like! We live in His presence and may suffer lack; why not live by His principle of faith and take back your dreams and visions from the devourer.

True faith is not the product of reason. It has nothing to do with human logic or the five senses such as hearing, tasting, seeing, feeling, or smell. The following scriptures prove that faith can grow. It is our responsibility to develop our faith. We must make the decision to depend on the finished work of Christ rather than depend on our reasoning. Faith can grow from weak faith to strong faith: Listed below are several levels of faith.

- Little faith [Luke 12:28]

- Weak faith [Romans 4:19]

- Strong faith [Romans 4:20

- Perfect faith [James 2:22]

- Overcoming faith [1 John 5:4]

- Great Faith [Matthew 8:10]

- Growing faith [2 Thessalonians 1:3]

Faith can be increased by:

1. Reading and studying the Bible.

2. Meditating and confessing scripture so that it becomes a part of your belief system.

3. Exercising your faith by putting the words you read into practice in your daily life.

4. Focusing on and believing what the Word says, not your feeling and emotions.

5. Understanding what Jesus has done and will do through you, not your own strength.

6. Asking the Holy Spirit to teach, lead, and guide you.

7. Praying in your prayer language.

8. Remembering what your faith has accomplished in the past.

The God Kind of Faith

The God kind of faith is motivated by love. *"But God commanded His love in that while we were yet sinners, Christ died for us." [Romans 5:8]* Without faith you can't please God, but without love you can't know Him at all. Love filled with faith and truth is the ultimate weapon against oppression, corruption, temptation and sin. Love must be the foundation for everything we do. Without it power can lead to pride and self-inflation. Love is the greatest truth of all. Love is what causes us to live in the Spirit, and it motivates our faith. True supernatural faith flows from the heart. It causes natural things to line up with what God has already accomplished spiritually.

This Scripture is one of the greatest promises for operating in faith. Jesus said, *"For assuredly I say to you whosoever says to this mountain, be removed and be cast into the sea, and does not doubt in his heart, but believes that those things he says will be done, he will have whatsoever he says. Therefore I say unto you, what things you desire, when you pray, believe that you receive them, and you shall have them." [Mark 11:23-24]* Great faith which is the God kind of faith moves God.

Little faith does not move a mountain of drugs, alcohol, pornography, abuse, depression, sickness, and disease. Great faith will move your mountain of lack, fear, and doubt or whatever is standing between you and total restoration. Listed below are six keys to release Kingdom faith:

1. The supernatural power of God and the Word activated by faith will operate together on your behalf.

2. Your words spoken in faith have power on earth to influence heaven on your behalf. However, a double-minded person is unstable in all his ways, and let him expect nothing of God.

3. Without faith, it is impossible to please God.

4. True faith will believe God's Word and will not waiver until the dream manifests.

5. Jesus is the source, author, developer, and finisher of our faith.

6. Faith is produced in the heart and released out of the mouth. Say to your mountain, "Move!"

Great faith is empowered by the anointing. The power for a healing anointing will manifest if you are praying for sick people to be healed. You must be intentional while looking for opportunities in which this anointing will be needed. *"Faith without works is dead." [James 2:20]*

The God kind of faith is an anointing to help people in a supernatural way and in the process will reveal God's heart to them. Don't allow yourself to become discouraged. No matter what you encounter, set your vision higher. Know and understand that God wants His people restored and renewed. Allow your faith to move you to action. This action will release the power of God to produce the miraculous. God doesn't work the same way every time so listen for his direction in each situation.

The God kind of faith is released within us through prayer and fasting. The disciples could not cure an epileptic boy, but Jesus did. [Matthew 17:14-21] When Jesus was asked why the disciples had no success, He said it was because of their unbelief. It wasn't a question of God's will. Jesus did not focus on the boy's faith, but His own faith. It was the level of faith within the disciple's heart that caused doubt. Jesus also pointed out that this kind does not go out except by prayer and fasting which Jesus did on a regular basis.

Prayer and fasting help release the God kind of faith within us. It is the faith principle that produces the miracle, not the fasting. Through prayer and fasting, we tap into the fullness of faith that exists in God's heart which is extended to us. It isn't by our works, but by God's faith and grace released toward us.

The God kind of faith is based on His Word alone, not your feelings. Anyone can believe what he can see, hear or feel in the natural. The God kind of faith is a spiritual gift from God. He has given us the measure of faith to allow us to receive salvation which is a rebirth of the human spirit. God's Word is true regardless of our feelings. Faith is a strong conviction that the promises of God are true.

The God kind of faith never allows present circumstances to diminish what God has said. You have to decide who you will believe. No matter what people say to discourage you, your words, thoughts, and actions must remain fixed on His words to you. The power of faith is based on consistency. *"If ye continue in faith, grounded and settled, and be not moved from the hope of the gospel, which ye have heard, and which was preached to every creature which is under heaven; whereof I Paul am made a minister."* [1 Colossians 1:23] KJV Determine today to be consistent. Day by day stand on the Word and tomorrow get up and stand on it again. There is power in consistent faith.

Unfortunately, people waiver in their faith walk. The devil quickly steals the promises that God placed in their heart. If Satan allows God's Word to stay alive in you, he knows he will lose; therefore, he has to bring problems, confusion, and doubt to destroy your peace, your hope, and your vision to make you compromise the promises spoken to you.

Faith fails when people see themselves as weak, depressed, oppressed, disabled, impoverished and slow to speak God's word about the situation. The concern with unstable faith is that it emanates from the flesh or five senses and not from the Spirit realm. Flesh says I'm broke, I'll never make it, or I can't eat or shop there. Real faith says I delight myself in the Lord, He will give me the desires of my heart, and my God shall supply all my needs according to His riches in glory by Christ Jesus.

Did you know that when a person belittles himself or herself, he or she is really criticizing God's workmanship? Can the clay say to the potter why did you make me this way? The God kind of faith believes what the Word says: *"For we are God's workmanship, created in Christ to do good works, which God prepared in advance for us to do. For you created my innermost being. You knit me together in my mother's womb. I will praise thee; for I am fearfully and wonderfully made: marvelous are thy works; and that my soul knows right well."* [Ephesians 2:10; Psalm 139:]

The God kind of faith is hindered when you believe in what you feel more than what Jesus taught in His Word. Anyone can believe in the natural- what he hears, sees, or feels. Faith is a spiritual gift from God that will give us the courage to stand up and fight for the will of God to be fulfilled. He has given each one of us the measure of faith. Faith is the very seed that grew inside until we received salvation, a rebirth of the human spirit. Natural or physical senses have nothing to do with the Bible. Jesus is the Way, the Truth, and the Life regardless of how we feel.

The world judges the Christian's faith walk when trials come. Your children, your husband or wife, your co-workers, and your friends know your level of faith because they listen to what comes out of your mouth. Change your words and change your life. Your faith will never rise above the words you speak. The Bible tells us to walk by faith and not by sight. Faith that is based on feelings and emotions will let you down when real trouble comes.

The God kind of faith will keep you when everything else fails. God tested Abraham's faith. Remember, faith not tested is faith not manifested. Your faith must pass the test before it can manifest what God has for you. God knew what was in Abraham's heart, but He still tested him so that Abraham would know that he possessed the God kind of faith. Until Abraham put his faith to the test by accepting God's will to sacrifice His son, Isaac, his faith was not manifested. Abraham was approved by God to build the next kingdom family once he proved that he would not withhold anything from God. Then God was able to bless Abraham to become the Father of many nations.

Abraham was willing to put the God kind of faith into practice:

- Resist all fear and oppression and fear that is coming against you. [2 Timothy 1:7]

- Defeat all symptoms of sickness in your body.[1Peter 2:24]

- Overcome worry by choosing to trust God in everything. [Philippians 4:6-7]

- Be willing to leave the familiar to create the unknown. [Romans 8:2]

- Live daily in God's safety and protection.[2Thess. 3:3]

- Be fully persuaded that God will do what He said He would do. [[Romans 4:20-21]

- Praise God in faith before the manifestation of the promise. [Romans 4:20]

- Have unshakable confidence that God will do the impossible on your behalf. [Romans 4:20-21]

- Rely on Divine revelation knowledge rather than your five senses. [Matthew 16:13-190]

- Wisdom and knowledge shall be freely given by the Spirit. [Isaiah 33:6]

The God kind of faith meditates on God's word, not idle words. Satan wants you to compromise your faith and take the easy way out of a difficult situation. Until you make a mark in the sand and refuse to be moved, you will continue to give in and give up. You will remain a person of little faith and allow the enemy to rule over you.

1. *"This Book of the law (God's principles or predictable outcomes) shall not depart from your mouth, but you shall meditate in it day and night, that you may observe to do according to all that is written therein. For then you will make your way prosperous, and then you will have good success." [Joshua 1:8]*

   To meditate on the Word means to ponder, to dwell on, and to consider; also to fix your mind on God's word, to chew on and digest, as well as to focus your attention on God's promises, not on life's problems.

2. *"Blessed is the man who walks not in the counsel of the ungodly, nor stands in the path of sinners, nor sits in the seat of the scornful; but his delight is in the law of the Lord, and in His law he meditates day and night. He shall be like a tree planted by the rivers of waters that brings forth its fruit in its seasons, whose leaf also shall not wither; and whatever he does shall prosper." [Psalm 1:1-3]*

The God kind of faith is reserved exclusively for born-again believers. The Holy Spirit has put God's faith into our hearts to have access to Him. Your faith in God puts you in the "God Class" when you stand firmly committed to faith principles.

The prayer of those in the "God Class" will always pray for the solution to a problem and not focus on the problem. I believe the principles of God will manifest in our schools our government, on the job, and elsewhere when true believers speak God's words of life to every situation.

❖

FAITH THAT HEALS

God wants us to be healed and healthy. He wants us to walk in Divine health which is the reason God programmed faith for healing into our DNA to empower and to promote our well-being. The New Testament informs born again Christians that we are already healed. *"Who Himself bore our sins in His own body on the tree, that we having died to sins, might live for righteousness by whose stripes you were healed."* [1st Peter 2:24]

The following is a blueprint for healing:

- Make sure there is no sin in your life. *"If we confess our sins, He is faithful and just to forgive us our sins and to cleanse us from all unrighteousness."* [1 john 1:9]

- Forgive others so you can be forgiven. *"And whenever you stand praying, if you have anything against anyone, forgive them, that your Father in Heaven may also forgive your trespasses."* [Mark 11:25]

- Have Scriptures to reinforce your faith. *"Now this is the confidence we have in Him, that if we ask anything according* to His will, He hears us. And if we know that He hears us, whatever we ask, we know that we have the petitions that we have asked of Him." [1 John 5:14, 15]

- Be prepared to believe you will receive. "Therefore I say to you, whatever things you ask when you pray, believe that you receive them, and you will have them." [Mark 11:24]

- Be prepared to immediately act in faith. "For as the body without the spirit is dead, so faith without works is dead also." [James 2:26]

- See yourself healed. "While we do not look at the things which are seen, but at the things which are not seen. For the things which are seen are temporary, but the things which are not are eternal." [2 Corinthians 4:18]

- Release your faith. "Jesus said unto him, 'Go your way; your son lives.' So the man believed the word that Jesus spoke to him…The father knew that it was at the same hour in which Jesus said to him, 'Your son lives.' And he himself believed, and his whole household." [John 4:50, 53]

- Begin to thank God for it… "With thanksgiving let your requests be made known to God." Philippians 4:6]

After praying for healing:

➢ Meditate daily on healing scriptures.

➢ Refuse to have doubt and fear about your healing.

- ➢ Continue to boldly confess your faith for healing.

- ➢ Also remain steadfast and resist the devil, in Jesus' name.

- ➢ Refuse all lying symptoms that try to come back on your body.

- ➢ Attend church regularly.

- ➢ Listen to messages that teach on healing.

I believe the enemy works especially hard to sabotage faith for healing. He knows that most often flesh has a low tolerance for pain which can devastate the entire person including the mind, will, emotions, and spiritual well-being. The enemy uses fear and doubt to drive the individual to make a quick decision based on the doctor's report before considering all the options. I believe that God heals through medical technology as well, but most often a walk of faith will establish deeper intimacy, stronger faith, and a sharper mind that will thrust you into the next level of your kingdom assignment.

The only reason we don't receive our answer to prayer is that we quit praying too soon. When our faith reaches the level where we can receive the answer, our bodies will be healed. Are you willing to spend the time in prayer to allow your faith to pull the answer out of the Spirit realm into the natural realm? The whole time we are praying, we need to believe that we have received the answer based on God's Word. I experienced this kind of faith building process several years ago when I asked God to heal my back.

Sometimes healing is a process instead of an instant miracle by the laying on of hands. My healing came in steps. First, I had to realize that God loved me enough to heal me like others in the Bible. I had to realize that I was as valued and significant as anyone else to God. Next, I had to speak my healing into existence by daily sending faith into the Spirit realm to pull healing into my body. Eventually, I knew I was healed because I could see myself healed in the Spirit realm. Now all I had to do was proclaim my healing until it manifested in my body.

My Prayers and healing Scriptures brought the desired results when I activated the God kind of faith instead of allowing fear and doubt to rule over me! Give the devil no place! The minute you feel pain, rebuke it right then and there! Faith worked for me and faith will do the same for you. God does not esteem one person above another. Amen?

"Peace to you! As the Father has sent Me, I also send you..." He breathed on them, and said to them, "Receive the Holy Spirit."

[John 20:22]

Eight

ENCOUNTERING THE SUPERNATURAL

One of the most profound and distinctive revelations of the whole Bible is that of the person and the work of the Holy Spirit. The world has a desire to seek the unknown from the dark side such as movies with themes based on the power of super heroes and scientific amazement. As Christian believers, we know that the power of the Gospel is revealed by God who is one, yet He is more than one. The three persons revealed in Scripture are the Father, the Son, and the Holy Spirit. Because of human parallels, it is comparatively easy to realize that God the Father is a person, and God the Son is a person, but it may not be as easy to realize that the Holy Spirit is also a person.

The Holy Spirit was part of all things from the very beginning of Scripture to the very end of Scripture. In the beginning "God." [Genesis 1:1] The term God in Hebrew is Elohim which means Godhead, a plural noun that stands for three persons, God the Father, God the Son, and God the Holy Spirit. The Holy Spirit co-exists with the Trinity. *"And the Holy Ghost (also called the Holy Spirit) descended in bodily shape like a dove upon Jesus, and a voice came from heaven, which said, Thou art my beloved Son; in thee I am well pleased."* [Luke 3:22] KJV

These three operate together in perfect harmony. It's good to know they never had a crisis management meeting in heaven, nor have they had a power struggle among themselves. The Holy Spirit is now the personal representative of the Godhead on earth. God the Father is in Heaven and the Lord Jesus is at the Father's right hand. The Holy Spirit is on earth to help us live victorious lives. As God's agent on earth, He is continuing the ministry of Jesus Christ.

The outpouring of the Holy Spirit at Pentecost reveals that the miraculous power of God was never intended to disappear from our lives or from the church, rather we are to increase more and more until Jesus comes. As believers, we live in His presence, and we are daily motivated by His extravagant love and power. Benny Hinn, Kenneth Copeland, and other mega church pastors are not the only ones who should be flowing in the supernatural anointing. God wants the outpouring of the Holy Spirit to come upon "ALL FLESH."

God's end time revival speaks of a great increase of salvations with an increase of believers being baptized in the Holy Spirit. *"And when the day of Pentecost was fully come, they were all with one accord in one place. And suddenly there came a sound from heaven as a rushing mighty wind, and it filled all the house where they were sitting. And there appeared unto them cloven tongues like as of fire, and it sat upon each of them. And they were all filled with the Holy Ghost, and began to speak with other tongues, as the Spirit gave them utterance." [Acts 2: 1-4]* KJV The Holy Spirit fell upon them suddenly baptizing and empowering the 120 disciples who prayed, fasted, and waited several days for God to supernaturally change them.

Jesus depended totally on the power of the Holy Spirit for His teaching and ministry. Now if Jesus needed the Holy Spirit, how much more do we need Him. The disciples were empowered to do mighty works after receiving the Holy Spirit. The Holy Spirit is the *Pneuma* which is the breath or wind of God.

"And when He had said this, He breathed on them, and said unto them; Receive ye the Holy Ghost." [John 20:22] We will have no effect on the world without the power of the Holy Spirit. Without Him, we can do nothing, but with Him all thing are possible! *"But ye shall receive power, after the Holy Ghost (Spirit) is come upon you: and ye shall be witnesses unto Me both in Jerusalem, Judea, and in Samaria, and unto the uttermost parts of the earth. [Acts 1:8] KJV*

The prophecy for the last days proclaims that there will be a greater manifestation of signs, and wonders, miracles, and gifts of the Holy Spirit. We need to honor the Holy Spirit by giving Him pre-eminence and lordship in our worship services, and allow Him to move and manifest His presence and power. He is here to give us the enablement to do what we can't do on our own.

- He is here to pour out His anointing on all flesh.

- The Holy Spirit is here to continue the ministry of Jesus through teaching, preaching, healing, manifesting signs, wonders, and miracles.

- The Holy Spirit is present to confirm, endorse, and demonstrate the message of God's Word.

- He comes to charge the atmosphere with His anointing.

- He comes to manifest the works of Jesus.

- He comes to release His supernatural gifts.

- He comes to saturate us with His presence.

❖

THE HOLY SPIRIT- OUR REVELATOR

The Holy Spirit is the interpreter, the revelator, and administrator of all that the Father and the Son have. The Bible says, *"When the Spirit of truth comes, He will guide you into all truth. He will not speak on His own, but will tell you what he has heard. He will tell you about the future. He will bring Me glory by telling you whatever he receives from Me. All that belongs to the Father is mine; this is why I said; The Spirit will tell you whatever He receives from Me."* [John 16:13-15] NIV All is revealed, interpreted, and administrated by the Holy Spirit. Jesus sent another person to take His place in the earth.

The Holy Spirit will reveal to you what is to come on a daily basis if you pray, ask for guidance, and obey Him. I recall one morning as I went out to meet with other witnesses to do street ministry, I saw a young man running toward the shopping center where I was soon to witness. As usual, we witnessed salvation to several people and prayed for healing and deliverance for others. I noticed that a few stores down, a young man sat by the grocery store rocking and asking for alms. I approached him and began to tell him how much Jesus loved him and wanted to bless his life in every area of need. He really wasn't listening to me, and he began to yell out to me that he was hungry. Then I remembered that he was the same person that I saw earlier running down the street.

I refused to allow this deception to overrule what I needed to say. A boldness came over me, and I told him that I saw him running earlier, and that his needs had already been supplied by God's kindness and mercy. I further stated that the enemy wanted to make him a cripple and a beggar when he should be proclaiming the goodness of God. He began to confess that he lived with his sister who worked, and that he received a disability check, but he daily begged for money to have extra cash. I asked him to stand up, and ask God to forgive him, and to stop allowing the devil to curse what God has blessed. My partners and I prayed for him, and I bought his lunch. He promised to discontinue trying to deceive people.

Several days later, I saw that same young man in the shopping center, but he was not sitting down or begging for food or money. If the Holy Spirit had not given me the enablement to challenge that young man's thinking, he would have no doubt continued to allow greed to control him. The Holy Spirit will teach you how to speak to others and tell you what to say in a loving, truthful manner. He will teach you to run to people, not away from them. Never forget that everything we do has to be motivated first by love. Sometimes a kind word spoken in love can restore a life, and cover a multitude of sin. [1Peter 4:8]

The Holy Spirit is our helper which is paraclete in the Greek language, and He is our advocate. A paraclete is someone who can do something for you that you can't do for yourself. The word advocate is derived from Latin which means lawyer. It means someone who speaks in our defense. We know the logos meaning of the word advocate, but spiritually, the Holy Spirit interprets for us the things we do not understand. In Heaven,

Jesus prays for us as our advocate and pleads our cause with the Father, and on earth, we have the Holy Spirit to do the same.

Jesus wanted the disciples to know that He would not abandon them. He told them this, *"And I will ask the Father, and He will give you another advocate, who will never leave you. He is the Holy Spirit who leads us into all truth. The world cannot receive Him, because it isn't looking for Him and doesn't recognize Him. But you know Him, because He lives with you now and later will be in you. No, I will not abandon you as orphans. I will come to you. Soon the world will no longer see Me, but you will see me. Since I live, you will also live."* [John 14: 16-19] NLT

Several promises were made in these verses. First, Jesus said that the Father will send you another Comforter. When Jesus was transfigured, He sent another person. In other words, Jesus exchanged places with the Holy Spirit for our good. While He was on earth, in His body, Jesus could only be one place at a time. He was limited by time and space. Now that the Holy Spirit is here, He can be everywhere at the same time, unlimited by time and space. As our High Priest, Jesus lets us know that we will not be left here without a *paraclete* which means advocate, attorney, comforter, counselor, and helper.

Then He said, "He will stay with you forever." In other words, He reminded the disciples that He had been with them three and a half years. He has to leave them, and He didn't want them to be heartbroken. Someone else will come who will never leave. The Holy Spirit is the exchange agent for Jesus. He also tells the disciples, "He lives with you and will be in you." The advocate and comforter will take up residence in you. "I will not leave you as orphans." Jesus lets us know that He has not abandoned us. He wants us to know that someone will always be here to care for us. Jesus then said, "I will come to you." This is important to know that we continue to experience His presence as He comes back to us unlimited by time and space in the Holy Spirit.

Immediately after the Holy Spirit came, those who received Him realized three new results:

1. They understood the plan of God and the ministry of Christ far better than they did when He was on earth. They could comprehend His love and compassion for the people.

2. Second, they became extremely bold. After the resurrection, they ran away from Jesus, locked their doors, and feared what the Jews might do to them. They were not willing or equipped to stand up to preach and proclaim the truth. However, the moment the Holy Spirit came to them on the Day of Pentecost, they changed. Peter boldly told the Jewish people in Jerusalem the whole story of Jesus, and placed the guilt of the crucifixion on them.

3. They had supernatural confirmations. The moment the Holy Spirit came, miracles began to happen. It was like Jesus was there with them again in person like He explained previously. "When the Holy Spirit comes, I'll come back in Him. I will be with you. I will not leave you as orphans."

YOUR SUPERNATURAL DNA

It is a powerful revelation to every believer to know that the Baptism of the Holy Spirit is part of the conversion or salvation experience. However, there are many Christians who claim that a "second infilling" of the Holy Spirit empowered them to operate with boldness. This power is for the purpose of preaching the Gospel, witnessing, and having a deeper devotion to God by living a sanctified life. Often, this infilling is accompanied by speaking in tongues. [Acts 4:31; Acts 2 :2-4]

Jesus commanded that the disciples receive the Holy Spirit. *"And when He had said this, He breathed on them, and said to them, "Receive the Holy Spirit."* [John 20:22] The Bible says that God spared not his own Son, but delivered Him up for us all, how shall He not freely give us all things? Seek the next level in your Christian growth by asking the Holy Spirit to give you power to witness to the lost with conviction, and to resurrect you from dead things around you that keep you bound. The enemy doesn't mind you living in God's presence as long as he can make you deny that you have the power of God living on the inside. The Holy Spirit wants to transform our words, our thoughts, our character, and our nature until it replicates the personhood of Christ.

Every believer can and must live with the compelling influence of the Holy Spirit if change is to occur. This can be realized as we hide the Word of God in our hearts with the truth of the teaching of Christ for the glory of God. The primary way the Holy Spirit works in the life of the believer is through the instruction and influence of the Word of God. The Holy Spirit will cultivate an understanding in the believer's heart to help the person conform to the truth being taught. It is difficult to live and speak the truth when you only have a "spiritual feeling" without the power of the spoken word. Move beyond emotional feelings to action.

My own experience supports the idea that the baptism of the Holy Spirit can be a secondary occurrence to salvation. Many years after becoming a Christian, I had experiences where the Holy Spirit moved upon me with great power. The result was a strong desire to study God's word, to pray more especially for the sick, to witness to people on the streets, to preach and teach the Gospel, to pray in tongues, and to listen to on-going praise music. I know that I began to experience a new depth in Christ that I had not noticed until the laying on of hands for me to receive the Holy Spirit.

I see too many Christians who merely exist without the desire to make a difference in their lives or the lives of others. One can rarely distinguish them from unbelievers. Their conversation is negative, and they usually discuss their hopeless condition and poor health, yet their spiritual DNA says they can do mighty works in Christ. It was the Holy Spirit that first led you to receive salvation. Now let Him baptize you with power and with fire. *"For our God is a consuming fire."* [Hebrews 12:29] KJV God's fire is to purify us, to draw people back to Him, to restore us back to His divine nature, not to torment us forever. Hell's fire is reserved for Satan and his followers, not Christians. [Malachi 3:23]

The Holy Spirit's function is to remind and to teach. Whatever the disciples needed to know, the Holy Spirit Himself brought it to their remembrance. The Holy Spirit reminded them of what Jesus had already taught, and He taught them what they needed to know about the Word of God which is also true for us today. Whatever we need to know about the Word, the Holy Spirit is here to teach us. The Holy Spirit is the author of Scripture, and He instructs us to understand the Word and to remember the Word, but we have to read in order to know what the Bible says. Remember, He is our helper!

The Holy Spirit is our own personal teacher and interpreter of Scripture. The revealing of the Scripture came to disciples on the day of Pentecost. The unbelieving crowd called them drunk, but Peter stood up and said: *"These are not drunk, as you suppose. It's only nine o'clock in the morning! No this is what was spoken by the prophet Joel..." [Acts 2:15-16]* NIV Peter received this revelation from the Holy Spirit that gave him an understanding of what had taken place in the upper room.

The apostle who had been persecuting the church and rejecting the teachings of Jesus also had an immediate transformation after the Holy Spirit came to him. *"Then Ananias went to the house (where Paul was) and entered it. Placing his hands on Saul, he said, 'Brother Saul, The Lord who appeared to you on the road as you were coming here has sent me so that you may see again and be filled with the Holy Spirit."[Acts 9:17]*

Immediately after that, Paul (before named Saul) began to preach in the synagogues that Jesus was the Son of God. The moment he received the Holy Spirit, he had a totally different understanding. He truly received new sight both physically and spiritually. He was transformed immediately because the Holy Spirit who is the author and teacher of Scripture was already in him.

The Holy Spirit is the interpreter and revelator of Scripture while Jesus is the personal Word of God and the Bible is the written Word of God. They all work together in perfect harmony. Jesus knew what the Holy Spirit would do when He came. Jesus said, *"I have much more to say to you, more than you can now bear. But when He, the Spirit of Truth comes, He will guide you into all truth. He will not speak on His own; He will speak only what He hears, and He will tell you what is yet to come. He will bring glory to Me by taking from what is mine and making it known to you. All that belongs to the Father is mine. That is why I said the Spirit will take from what is mine and make it known to you."* [John 16:12-15] NIV

The Holy Spirit reveals Jesus in His totality. He glorifies Jesus and reveals every aspect of the nature character, and ministry of Jesus.

The Holy Spirit is the foundation of the ministry concerning the church. This is a list of a few of His functions in the body of Christ:

- The Holy Spirit formed the universal church. [Ephesians 2:19-20]

- The Holy Spirit desires to inspire the worship service. [Philippians 3:3]

- The Holy Spirit gives us a new prayer language. [Mark 16:17]

- The Holy Spirit gives gifts to believers to advance His ministry. [1Corinthians 12:7]

- He desires to direct the church's missionary work. [Acts 13:2-4]

- He wants to influence songs of praise and worship. [Ephesians 5:18]

- He desires to appoint its preachers. [1Corinthians 2:4]

- He wants to warn members of what's to come. [1 timothy 4:1]

- He helps to determine right decisions. [Acts 15:28]

- He seeks to organize the church's evangelistic efforts. [Acts 1:8]

❖

THE HOLY SPIRIT AS INTERCESSOR

The Holy Spirit helps us to pray fervent and effective prayers. In order to live as a mature Christian, you must be led continually by the Spirit of God. *"For as many as are led by the Spirit of God they are the sons of God…The Spirit itself bears witness with our spirit that we are the children of God."* [Romans 8:14-16] KJV

The Holy Spirit guides our prayer life to help us pray meaningful prayers. Paul said, *"And in the same way the Spirit also helps our weakness; for we do not know how to pray as we should, but the Spirit Himself intercedes for us with groaning too deep for words; and He who searches the hearts knows what the mind of the Spirit is because he intercedes for the saints according to the will of God."* [Romans 8:26-27]

The mind, not the physical body, has a weakness when it comes to prayer. We do not always know how to pray or what to pray.

The key to effective praying is learning how to relate to, and submit to the Holy Spirit. Then we can let Him guide, direct, inspire, strengthen, and actually pray through us. One way the Holy Spirit intercedes for us is with groaning too deep for words. Our limited minds do not have the words to express what needs to be prayed. That's when the Holy Spirit prays through us in a very sacred experience or a travail that leads to spiritual birth or manifestation of a thing. No real spiritual reproduction in the church occurs without spiritual travail in prayer according to Paul: *"My dear children, for whom I am again in the pains of childbirth until Christ is formed in you..." [Galatians 4:19] NIV*

Another way in which the Holy Spirit helps us in prayer is that He illuminates our minds. He doesn't actually pray through us, but He shows us in our minds what we need to pray for and how we need to pray for it. The Holy Spirit moves in and renews the mind. Only a renewed mind can find out God's will first, in order to pray His will. The Holy Spirit helps us by transforming our minds from a carnal to a spiritual way of perceiving things by illuminating and revealing to us how we should pray.

The Holy Spirit helps us by putting the right words in our mouths. Have you ever prayed a pray filled with words that revealed exactly what you needed to say, and you were amazed at how everything came together so powerfully that you knew you could never repeat it? The Holy Spirit will show you His enablement when you trust Him in prayer. I remember praying for a young lady that I believed God was going to heal.

When I asked her what she needed, she suggested that I could pray that she would not have pain after surgery. The Holy Spirit told me to pray that she would not suffer pain because she did not have faith for an immediate miracle. It is difficult to pray for more than the person can believe. She had faith for less pain, but she did not have faith that she could be healed instantly. She later confirmed that she had a painless surgery. Praise the Lord!

The Holy Spirit gives us a new prayer language, one that the natural mind does not know. Paul said, *"For anyone who speaks in a tongue (an unknown language) does not speak to men but to God. Indeed no one understands him; he utters mysteries with his spirit. [1 Corinthians 14:2] NIV* This kind of prayer 1) Speaks directly to God, not to men, 2) Speaks what our minds do not understand- mysteries or sharing God's secrets, 3) Speaks to edify self, and to build up oneself. When we let the Holy Spirit in, yield to him, and let Him work in us according to scripture, there will be a new richness and variety in our prayer life. Holy Spirit assisted prayer pleases God.

❖

THE HOLY SPIRIT AND GOD'S DIVINE LOVE

The greatest and most wonderful of all the blessings of the Holy Spirit is the outpouring of God's Divine love in our hearts. You can't fake love. Most people can distinguish between genuine love and pretense. God's love is poured out in our hearts by the Holy Spirit. Love must be the foundation for everything we do. Experiencing the Father's loving embrace is taking hold of the deepest love you will ever experience and never letting go. We need to know that God wants to draw us close to His heart no matter what we are experiencing.

God loves us unconditionally. Through His love and Divine mercy, He gave His only Son to pay our sin debt and forgive us our sin debt and transgressions. He took upon Himself spiritually all our sins, all our diseases, all our infirmities, and sacrificed his life for us on the cross to give us eternal victory over death, hell and the grave. What a great love! For God so loved the world that He gave His one and only Son that whoever believes in Him shall not perish but have everlasting life. [John 3:16]

God's love is agape, the highest form of love. Agape loves whether or not the person deserves or returns that love. *"But God demonstrates His own love toward us, in that while we were yet sinners, Christ died for us." [Romans 5:8]* The Agape love of God is not just something that happens to you; it's something you make happen. Christ's love for us, the pattern for our love, is a sacrificial gift. Christ's love is unconditional, forgiving, kind, eternal, and sensitive to our needs. You can be saved, filled, healed, delivered, and anointed, but if you choose not to receive our Father's Divine love, you will continue to struggle with fears, insecurities, feeling of inferiority, loneliness, and emotional pain.

What I love about God is that He loves us equally, but it is up to each individual to accept the love He has poured out to us in the person of the Holy Spirit. It always brings me joy to feel His presence surrounding me when I pray, sing, study the Word, or even think about Him. There is no greater joy than to see my savior working through me at times to witness to the lost, pray for the sick, share encouraging words or to preach or teach the Gospel of Christ. There are Divine opportunities everywhere, but you have to open your spiritual eyes and allow the Holy Spirit to speak to your heart in order to use your gifts for the Kingdom.

I want to encourage you to believe that God is very concerned about every aspect of your life. He knows your needs, your desires, your dreams, your struggles, and your every circumstance and situation at this moment. You are walking with a supernatural God who will open doors for you that you can never open without Him. The Bible says with man this is impossible, but with God all things are possible. [Matthew 19:26]; *"For I am persuaded that neither death nor life, neither angels nor principalities (demons), nor powers, nor things present nor things to come, nor height nor depth, nor any other created thing, shall be able to separate us from the love of God which is in Christ Jesus our Lord."* [Romans 8: 38-39]

Our life in Christ is a finished work of love that gives every believer certain rights and privileges. When Jesus said, "It is finished," He was not referring to His death alone. He was also speaking of the completion of all things the Kingdom of God has in store for you and me. Your poverty and lack were finished. Your health and healing were finished. Your depression and low self-esteem were finished. Your fears, doubts, and unsuccessful attempts to excel were finished because you can continue until you reach your goal. In Christ you will always win! God has many new experiences for us to pursue, but make no mistake; the work of Christ is finished. He is seated with His Father interceding for you and me. God doesn't have to invent a solution to your problems because the answer is already available. However, you can't see it until you are ready to let Him show you a better way.

When you realize how much God loves you, your spiritual receptors will regain the ability to receive His truth instead of the world's lies.

1. You will see yourself as God sees you.

2. You will know who you are in Christ.

3. You will hear with spiritual ears and see with spiritual eyes.

4. You will receive what Christ has done for you through His finished work on the cross.

5. You will rise up with confidence to continue the earthly ministry of Christ.

❖

THE GIFTS OF THE HOLY SPIRIT

The purpose of spiritual gifts is to help the church function more effectively by ministering to the needs of the body of Christ. God wants us to use these supernatural gifts not only inside the church but outside the church as well in supermarkets, department stores, hotels, restaurants, banks, gyms, and everywhere else. We are to be full of the Holy Spirit to minister wherever and whenever we are needed. God's gifts are perfect, but they are manifested through imperfect people like you and me.

Just as we have five physical senses that allow us to operate in the natural world, we also have the nine gifts of the Holy Spirit to minister in the Spirit realm. These gifts include three revelation gifts: Word of wisdom, Word of knowledge, and Discerning of Spirits. Three power gifts: Faith, Healings, and Miracles. Three inspirational gifts: Prophecy, Diverse tongues, and Interpretation of tongues.

"There are diversities of gifts, but the same Spirit. There are differences of ministries, but the same Lord. And there are diversities of activities, but it is the same God who works all in all: For to one is given the word of wisdom through the Spirit, to another the word of knowledge through the same Spirit, to another faith by the same Spirit, to another gifts of healings by the same Spirit, to another the workings of miracles, to another prophecy, to another discerning of spirits, to another different kinds of tongues, to another the interpretation of tongues. But one and the same Spirit works all these things, distributing to each one individually as He wills." [1 Corinthians 12:4-11] NKJV

God has given His people nine mighty gifts of the Holy Spirit to enable them to mature spiritually, edify others, and do the work of the ministry. Although these gifts of God are perfect, the manifestation of these gifts are sometimes not perfect because they operate through an imperfect channel: men and women. The DNA of God Himself has been placed in the church to continue the ministry of Jesus in the earthly kingdom until He returns. Pray that you receive and operate in your calling to the glory of God. The nine gifts of the Holy Spirit are further explained below:

1. A Word of Knowledge is conviction or a knowing that comes to you in a dream, vision, mental picture, or Scripture that deeply inspires you. It is supernatural insight by Divine enlightenment of situations or circumstances concerning the present. [Joshua 7:10-11]

2. The Word of Wisdom is the application of knowledge that God gives you. The gift of the word of wisdom reveals hidden, prophetic truths of the future. This gift involves

having a sense of Divine direction to accomplish God's will in a given situation. [1Corinthians 2:6-7]

3. The gift of Discerning of Spirits is the supernatural ability given by the Holy Spirit to perceive the source of a spiritual manifestation and determine whether it is of God, of the devil, of man or the world. The gift of the discerning of spirits is the supernatural power to detect the realm of the spirits and their activities. It is not psychic phenomena, or the ability to criticize and find fault. [Acts 10:30-35; 8:18-23]

4. The gift of Faith is the supernatural ability to believe God without doubt and unbelief. It is the ability to visualize what God wants to accomplish, and to meet adverse circumstances with trust in God's words and messages. It is the ability to believe for the miraculous. This gift not only operates in healings and miracles, but in the realm of the impossible as well. [John 9:1-7]

5. The gift of Healings refers to supernatural healing without human aid; it is a special gift to pray for specific diseases. God intervenes with his sovereign will and glory to work this miracle for us. There are three types of "gifts" of healings: physical (diabetes, cancer, deafness, etc.), emotional (jealousy, worry, discouragement and other destructive attitudes), and spiritual (bitterness, resentment, greed, guilt, etc.).

The gifts of Healing belong to all believers according to Mark 16:17-20. You can know whether you have the gift of healing by 1) the inner witness of the Holy Spirit [Romans 8:16], 2) a special ability to believe for physical healing [Romans 12:3-8], and 3) an overwhelming feeling of compassion which moves you to action. [Matthew 20:34]

6. The gift of the Working of Miracles is the supernatural power of God that intervenes in the ordinary course of events with exact timing to bring glory to God. A miracle is the performance of something which is against the laws of nature; it is the supernatural power to counteract earthly and evil forces. The word miracles comes from the Greek word dunamis which means "power and might that multiplies itself." Salvation is the greatest miracle. God expects us to utilize these gifts to bring non-believers to repentance in order to enlighten spiritually dead people so that they can be transformed into believers in Jesus Christ. [Acts 4:33, Mark 16:20]

7. The gift of Prophecy is a supernatural proclamation in a known language. Prophecy is a divinely inspired utterance that edifies, exhorts, and comforts. It builds us up, strengthens, and should lead us to the Word of God. It is the ministry of the Holy Spirit to convict people of sin, of righteousness, and of judgment to come. Prophecy is essentially forthtelling; it is a ministry to make people better and more useful Christians today. Prophecy in the New Testament church carries no prediction with it, but it edifies, exhorts, and comforts. Teaching and preaching are preplanned, prophecy is not. When a prophecy is given, we are to test it and hold on to what is good in it.

8. Diverse Tongues is a supernatural utterance through the power of the Holy Spirit in a person that manifests as spiritual language. These languages may be existent in the world, revived from some past culture, or unknown in the sense that they are a means of communication inspired by the Holy Spirit. Diverse tongues is the most misunderstood and dynamic gift. At Pentecost the church received the gift to communicate the gospel in foreign languages. [Acts 2]

9. Interpretation of Tongues is a supernatural verbalization and interpretation to reveal the meaning of a diverse tongue. This gift operates out of the mind of the Spirit rather than the mind of man. It is important to note that interpretation of tongues does not mean translation of tongues. You can ask God to move through you to give the interpretation so others will understand what was spoken. You can also ask the Father to interpret your own private prayers for your own personal benefit. The Word of God says that if you pray in tongues, you should pray that you will also interpret. [1Corinthians 14:27-28]

You cannot strengthen someone who is weak unless you are mature yourself. Spiritual gifts help you mature so that you can edify the church and strengthen others. Knowing that we have a gift to edify the body of Christ enables us to achieve a deeper level of self-acceptance and purpose in life. As we exercise our gifts, we experience personal fulfillment and a deep sense of joy. Spiritual gifts are given to edify the people of God, not to esteem oneself as more important than others.

"But you shall receive power when the Holy Spirit has come upon you: and you shall be witnesses to Me both in Jerusalem, and in Judea, and Samaria, and to the end of the earth."

[Acts 1: 8]

Nine

THE ANOINTING OF THE HOLY SPIRIT

The anointing is the manifest presence of God. One purpose of the Holy Spirit anointing, which comes in the baptism of the Holy Spirit, is to give us power to be Christ's witnesses. *"For John truly baptized with water, but you shall be baptized with the Holy Spirit not many days from now...."But you shall receive power when the Holy Spirit has come upon you; and you shall be witnesses to Me in Jerusalem, and in Judea and Samaria, and to the end of the earth."* [Acts 1:5; 2:8]NKJV

Many Christians fear witnessing because they think they have to do it with their own natural abilities or power. I have learned that when we put action to our faith, the Holy Spirit will operate through us. The more you cultivate an environment for God's presence, the more power you will have. The anointing will flow when we live in the Word and constantly renew our minds. Avoid things that would grieve the Holy Spirit. Knowledge of the Word is essential along with personal preparation in the areas of character, integrity, and holiness will enable you to have a constant flow of the anointing.

We must remember that the source of the anointing is God, and it is by His grace that we are qualified to be partakers of His glory. The Day of Pentecost was the fulfillment of John the Baptist's words about the Holy Spirit's baptizing with fire, and God confirmed the validity of the Holy Spirit's ministry at Pentecost.

"When the Day of Pentecost had fully come, they were all with one accord in one place. And suddenly there came a sound from heaven, as of a rushing mighty wind, and it filled the whole house where they were sitting. Then there appeared to them divided tongues, as of fire, and one sat upon each of them. And they were filled with the Holy Spirit and began to speak with other tongues, as the Spirit gave them utterance." [Acts 2:1-4] Tongues symbolize speech and the communication of the Gospel. Fire symbolizes God's purifying presence which burns away undesirable elements of our lives and sets our hearts aflame to ignite the lives of others.

The anointing comes for a reason and has an intended purpose. Jesus quoted these words as He spoke to the people in the synagogue. *"The Spirit of the Lord God is upon Me, because the Lord has anointed me to preach good tidings to the poor; He has sent Me to heal the brokenhearted, to proclaim liberty to the captives, and the opening of the prison to those who are bound; to proclaim the acceptable year of the Lord."* [Isaiah 61:1-2] In these verses, the five purposes of the anointing are revealed:

1. To enable you to preach the good news effectively. The anointing will enable you to share the Word with power.

2. To make you a messenger that proclaims freedom for the prisoners-freedom from the prison of sin, of drugs, of depression, and of dominating habits.

3. You are anointed to bring recovery of sight to the blind as Jesus did in His ministry.

4. You are anointed to release the oppressed. You have a message of release for people bound by sin and sickness, by demonic attacks and mental diseases.

5. You are anointed to proclaim the year of the Lord's favor to people unaware of the liberating message of God's grace.

The Holy Spirit anointing gives us power to go around doing good deeds. You know what happened in Judea, beginning in Galilee after the baptism that John preached, *"How God anointed Jesus of Nazareth with the Holy Spirit and power, and how He went around doing good and healing all who were under the power of the devil, because God was with Him."* [Acts 10:38]

The phrase "doing good" has several meanings. The Greek root for this phrase means benefactor or philanthropist, to bestow a benefit. In addition to the anointing for healing, delivering, preaching, witnessing, and miracle-working power, it is also to empower us to be givers, and to help needy people.

The anointing also gives you power to break the devil's yoke and to hear, discern, to teach, and to know the truth. *"But the anointing which you have received from Him abides in you, and you do not need that anyone teach you; but as the same anointing teaches you concerning all things, and is true, and is not a lie, and just as it has taught you, you will abide in Him."* [1 John 2:27]

Christ promised to send the Holy Spirit to teach His followers and remind them of all He had taught. As a result, Christians

Have the Holy Spirit anointing within them to keep them from going astray. Today, we also have the God-inspired Scriptures to instruct us as well. To stay true to Christ, we must follow the Word and His Spirit. This means we place our total trust in Christ and live as He wants us to live in a close personal relationship with Him.

❖

THE FIVE-FOLD MINISTRY ANOINTING

"And He Himself gave some to be apostles, some prophets, some evangelists, and some pastors and teachers." [Ephesians 4:11] The key is to find your place of ministry in the body of Christ. The anointing will follow your calling! Kathryn Kuhlman related that when you walk in the five-fold ministry, it may cost you everything. What is the price to pay?

- You have to deny yourself.

- You have to wait on God.

- You have to die to your plans and obey God's plans.

- You have to lay aside your will and follow God's perfect will.

- You have to pray, fast, seek God, worship, and live a holy life.

- You have to be obedient to God's voice, not man's.

The purposes of the five-fold ministry are: 1) For the equipping of the saints for the work of the ministry. 2) For edifying and building up the body of Christ. The anointing is power and the life force of God flowing through you for ministry. Without the anointing of the Holy Spirit, we have nothing to give people, sermons are dead words. We must rely one-hundred percent on the Holy Spirit to do the job of ministry.

Ministry is a walk of boldness. Peter witnessed to the lame man at the gate called Beautiful with boldness. [Acts 4:1-13] Boldness is not arrogance or loudness. Boldness means dare to do it. *"The wicked flee when no one pursues, but the righteous are as bold as a lion."* [Proverbs 28:1] If you believe God has called you for five-fold ministry, you should be bold in soul-winning, bold against Satan, bold to lay hand on, bold against sickness, fear, and oppression in order to help people.

There is a specific anointing that goes with each calling to help you destroy yolks that you may face in the five-fold ministry. A yolk is any kind of power, influence, force, or addiction. The anointing of God destroys every yolk- the yolk of religious tradition, depression, sin, sickness, resentment, criticism, control, demonic oppression, unforgiveness, sexual sins, pornography, and the like.

Jesus walked in all five ministry gifts without measure. God appointed Jesus to be the anointed head of the church. Jesus led captivity captive and gave these gifts to men to continue the Kingdom of God in the earth realm. If you are part of the five-fold ministry, you are expected to lead others to Christ and to teach them godly principles in order to equip the saints while building the body of Christ. A description of the office of the five-fold ministry anointing is as follows:

1. Apostle- A sent one who lays foundations for churches. The Apostle Paul also was a teacher and a pioneer that was motivated to start churches in new areas. An apostle has the vision to begin new projects.

2. The ministry gift of a Prophet is to hear the mind of God. The prophet has discernment, keeps us on track, and receives understanding, visions, and revelations from God. The prophet keeps us from acting in the flesh, and to be led by the Spirit. *"I say then: Walk in the Spirit, and you shall not fulfill the lust of the flesh. For the flesh lusts against the Spirit and the Spirit against the flesh: and these are contrary against one another, so that you do not do the things that you wish."* [Galatians 5:16-17]

3. The Evangelist proclaims the good news, wins the lost, heals the sick, teaches the saints about discipleship, and patches up the saints to get them believing in God again.

4. The Pastor/shepherd has the day-by-day care of the sheep and cares of the church. Pastors lead by example in attitude, word, and lifestyle. They show love and compassion for the sheep while feeding the flock of God.

5. Teachers/Ministers seek the lost, bind up the broken, minister healing to the sick, watch out for attacks that might scatter the sheep, strengthen those in bondage, proclaim the Gospel, and explain God's Word. The ministry gift of a teacher is to teach the saints what is expected of them

after they receive salvation. The teacher explains how to grow as believers and inspires others to become interested in learning what God expects of the believer. They also teach believers to study to show thyself approved unto God, a workman who need not be ashamed, rightly dividing the word of truth. [2nd Timothy 2:15]

As a minister and a teacher, I can attest to the fact that without the Holy Spirit anointing, I can do nothing on my own effort. Although I prepare an outline for my messages, I feel void until the Holy Spirit shows up, and He always does. I made an altar call after ministering one Sunday as the Holy Spirit had so instructed me to do even though I wasn't quite sure what might happen. I just boldly stepped out and asked that those who were sick, those who needed salvation, and those who wanted to be restored back to the church to come forth. I waited a moment for people to accept the invitation but there was no immediate response. Then I started to return to my seat when the pastor asked me to turn around. Suddenly, the altar was full of people.

As I laid hands on them and prayed for them, the Holy Spirit really began to manifest in that meeting. Most of them were slain in the Spirit, while others were crying and confessing Christ as their Lord and savior. The altar call is a special part of my ministry. I love to witness the visitation of the Spirit in the lives of those who reach out to Him. He will not fail or disappoint us.

Holy Father, I pray that today, every believer will receive a visitation from the Holy Spirit to be baptized in the Holy Spirit anointing for the call upon their life. I further decree and declare that a boldness will manifest and remain in them to help them witness to the lost, to destroy every yoke of the enemy, to minister healing and life to the sick, and to break the band of wickedness off those in bondage. I ask you to do these things in the Holy name of Jesus according to John 14:14, "If you ask anything in My name, I will do it." Amen

❖

HOW TO LIVE SPIRITUALLY

God's ultimate plan is to transform believers into the image of His Son, Jesus Christ. He wants to separate us from a carnal, worldly, nature and sanctify us completely- spirit, soul, and body. Sanctification is the continuous process of being made Holy resulting in a changed lifestyle for the believer. You have to invite the Holy Spirit to prune out all the negative qualities that your personality doesn't want you to release. Your hunger for a closer relationship will increase your desire to let the Holy Spirit tell you what to "take off" and what to "put on." Your total obedience is required for this deeper, spiritual work in you which will take you to a higher position in your calling for Kingdom purpose. *"Now may the God of peace sanctify you completely, and may your whole spirit, soul, and body be preserved blameless at the coming of our Lord Jesus Christ."* [1Thessalonians 5:23]

The following steps are basic to our spiritual growth in order to begin the sanctification process:

1. Make Jesus Christ Lord over every part of our lives, so that we have totally surrendered our lives to Him. [1st Samuel 12:24]

THE ANOINTING OF THE HOLY SPIRIT

2. Renounce every association with groups that do not confess Jesus as Lord and the Bible as the Word of God. [1st Thessalonians 1:9]

3. Receive and obey Christ's command and be baptized in water giving public testimony of our new life in Christ which identifies with His death, burial, and resurrection. [Matthew 28:19]

4. Read and study the Bible everyday to renew our mind, feed our spirit, and build our faith. [2nd Timothy 2:15; Matthew 4:4]

5. Spend time in prayer everyday: praise and worship, thanksgiving, intercession, and listening to God [James 5:16]

6. Get rid of and stay free from unforgiveness, resentment, bitterness, toward everyone. Unplug from hurtful memories, and plug into the promises of God.

"And whenever you stand praying, if you have anything against anyone, forgive him, that your Father in heaven may also forgive your trespasses. Forgiveness is not an emotion; forgiveness is a decision. [Mark 11:25-26]

1. Join a New Testament church that preaches God's Word and honors the Holy Spirit. [Hebrews 10:25]

2. Terminate wrong friendships and ungodly associations that hinder us, and form right relationships in the body of Christ. Do not allow friends to draw you back into a life of sin. [James 4:4]

3. Put on the whole armor of God and resist temptations by using the Word of God and the blood of Jesus. [1stCorinthians 10:13; Ephesians 6:10]

4. Honor the Lord with our finances by giving tithes and offerings to anointed ministers. [Proverbs 3: 9-10]

5. Receive the baptism in the Holy Spirit with the evidence of speaking in tongues. [Acts 2:1-4; Acts 1:8]

6. Be willing to grow spiritually, share our testimony and be a bold witness to win souls. [1stCorinthians 12:4]

"And God is able to make all grace abound toward you, always having all sufficiency in all things, may have an abundance for every good work."

[II Corinthians 9:8]

Ten

OPERATING IN KINGDOM PROSPERITY

I am convinced that God wants us to prosper in every way –spirit, soul, and body. Like any other parent, Father God wants His family to be healthy, happy, and successful. The first earthly family was created in His image, and they were given dominion over the earthly realm. God created man in His own image...then God said to them, be fruitful and multiply, fill the earth and subdue it; have dominion over the fish of the sea, over the birds of the air, and over every living thing that moves upon the earth. Even in the beginning, Adam and Eve had control of the entire estate called earth.

The enemy does not want us to use the power we possess over him. He wants us to forget that we are made in God's image with His DNA which makes us victors and not victims. He beguiled the first family and stole their inheritance; likewise, he desires to do the same thing to your family. When you know who you are in Christ, you will no longer be deceived. You will use you faith to stand on the immutable, infallible, invincible Word of God to prosper in every area of your life.

God wants to be our source of security in all areas of our lives including our finances. When we become rooted and grounded in God's truth and apply God's words to the situation, things will change. We will live in Divine health. We will overcome a poverty spirit, and we will stop the enemy's attacks. The devil is a thief and unless we arrest him for crimes against humanity, he will continue to destroy your present and future dreams and goals, your relationships, and especially your finances.

King David and his army were faced with a major attack at Ziklag; whereby, the enemy took their families and possessions. King David did three things before making a counterattack: 1) He encouraged himself, 2) He inquired of the Lord, 3) He attacked his enemies and recovered all. King David did not let the problem linger, nor did he plan a meeting with three other kings. He immediately fought back because he knew that Jehovah Nissi was on his side.

God always validates his promises and principles when we trust Him. *"And God is able to make all grace (favor and blessings) abound toward you, that you always having all sufficiency in all things, may have an abundance for every good work."* [2 Corinthians 9:8] NIV Whenever we see the rainbow in the sky, we are reminded of God's covenant with mankind that He is our source, and He will never leave us nor forsake us.

God's plan for our security covers the entire spectrum of all our needs. [Jeremiah 29:11] Prosperity from God's point of view is not only about finances, it also covers our mental, spiritual, and physical needs. As believers, we should be able to make this claim: We are born again and live daily under the Lordship of Jesus Christ. We have a sound mind that is free from fear, depression, oppression, and anxiety. We have God's peace, and we walk in Divine health, free from strife, unforgiveness, resentment, and jealousy. We are living in God's abundance; therefore, we give our tithes and offerings to bless the poor because our bills are paid.

Some traditional believers with a religious spirit want to distort God's Word by influencing Christians to deny their inheritance and choose to live beneath God's promises. Only those who learn to speak God's Words will have what He said they can have. God will not force us to receive His blessings. If you choose to have a spirit of poverty and lack, God will not override your decision; nevertheless, it is His will that we prosper and be in health as our soul prospers. [3 John: 2]

It is Father's will for us to inherit the blessings of Abraham. *"If you are Christ's, then you are Abraham's seed, and heirs according to the promise."* [Galatians 3:29] It is His will for you to be blessed which means to be well supplied with abundant provisions. [Proverbs 10:22]

Most Christians believe without a doubt that they are saved, but religious tradition makes them feel that prosperity is not for them. Scripture records these verses: You have dominion (broad scope of influence) on earth. *"You have made him to have dominion over the works of Your hands; You have put all things under his feet."* [Psalm 8:6] God gave the world to Jesus to rule over, and Jesus gave dominion to Christians. We are responsible to God for doing His will on earth.

God told Isaac about his inheritance and the inheritance of all nations. *"And I will make your descendants multiply as the stars of heavens. I will give your descendants all these lands, and in your seed all the nations of the earth shall be blessed. Because Abraham obeyed My voice and kept My charge, My commandments, My statutes, and My laws." [Genesis 26: 4-5]*

Our adversary, the devil, wants to hinder believers by making them deny the word "prosperity." He wants you to see your family struggling financially week after week and living in lack. He wants you to be depressed, worried, and always wondering if the world's financial system will continue to support those in dire straits. Satan knows that if he can keep Christians poor and churches behind in their budget, then he will hinder the financing of the Gospel and the outreach to save souls.

True prosperity is the wealth of the Kingdom which is the Word of God. Revelation knowledge goes beyond the natural realm. Real prosperity is using the Word of God by faith. The Holy Spirit operates inside to provide all that we need. *"The Kingdom is not meat and drink but righteousness and peace and joy in the Holy Ghost." [Romans 14:17]*

The Word tells us that we are blessed. *"Grace be to you and peace from God our Father and from the Lord Jesus Christ who has blessed us with all spiritual blessings in heavenly places in Christ." [Ephesians 1:3]* Spiritual blessings come from God to operate on our behalf in natural conditions. Most of us can agree that God has moved in a miraculous ways to bless us in times of persecution and distress. Daniel released his faith to shut the mouths of lions. Isaac released faith to sow and receive in the same year 100 times as much as he planted. Ruth's faith led her to a new land of promise where she met her Boaz. Having been justified by Christ, we are joint-heirs with Him. We are already seated in heavenly places awaiting the day of His triumphant return to restore all things.

All of heaven's provisions are ours now. *"In Him we have obtained an inheritance, being predestined according to the purpose of Him who works all things according to the counsel of His will.; [Ephesians 1:11]* Our real prosperity is having all of our needs met through faith in Christ, the Anointed One by means of the Holy Spirit.

As believers, we can trust God to supply every need because He has chosen us in Him before the foundation of the world. [Ephesians 1:4] The moment God created mankind, He set aside every provision we would ever need to operate in the earthly kingdom. He taught us to pray and believe that the kingdom will come on earth as it is in heaven. Heaven has no poverty, sickness, death or sorrow. We look forward to that day when the earthly kingdom will also operate in His presence and His principles forever.

About the Author

Dr. Susanna (Susie) Moore Gentry-Bell was born in Blanch, North Carolina, a small town in Caswell County where she attended elementary and high school. Dr. Bell received her Bachelor of Arts Degree in Language Arts from North Carolina Central University in Durham, NC., and Master Degrees in Education and Counseling from North Carolina A&T State University in Greensboro, NC. Dr. Bell also received a Ph.D. in Clinical Christian Counseling and Ministerial Ordination and Licensure from the National Christian Counseling Association and Jacksonville Theological Seminary in Jacksonville, Florida.

Susanna M. G. Bell, Ph.D., is a licensed pastoral counselor, an ordained minister, and a board-certified state and national counselor in mental and behavioral health. She is a former secondary school educator and counselor. As an ordained minister and psychotherapist, Dr. Bell is committed to strengthening individuals and families from a holistic premise that seeks to restore balance physically, mentally, and spiritually.

In addition to her role as a psychotherapist, Dr. Bell ministers at various churches, and conferences where she shares her message of empowerment, and significance through the indwelling power of a loving God. Her desire is to minister inner healing and purpose to individuals in order to help them fulfill their Kingdom assignment in Christ.

Today, Dr. Bell is the founder and director of Restoration Counseling Ministries located in Brown Summit, North Carolina, in Guilford County. She continues to provide therapy to her clients in a compassionate, therapeutic setting. She is the mother of three sons, and the grandmother of three lovely granddaughters.

As a recently appointed World Peace Ambassador, Dr. Bell joins the Universal Peace Federation which promotes peace initiatives both nationally and internationally across a broad spectrum of cultures and nations throughout the world.

Dr. Susanna M. G. Bell's Contact Information:
Website: www.restcounselingministries.vpweb.com
Email: sm_bell@bellsouth.net or info@restcounselingministries.vpweb.com
Office: (336) 656.7416

Book Orders: https://www.createspace.com/4552946

A SEVEN DAY INTERCESSORY PRAYER JOURNAL

Pray an intercessory prayer each day of the week in order for God's security, protection, and provisions to cover each individual on your prayer list.

Heavenly Father, it is written in Psalm 91, and other scriptures also that You are our Deliverer, and I ask that You give everyone I pray for today total victory in every area of need. I pray that they receive total deliverance, freedom, liberty, and salvation from all evil, wicked, lying, unclean and perverse spirits; total victory from sickness, diseases, infirmities, afflictions, infections, and disorders of any kind in every cell of their bodies. I ask You Lord to remove abnormal growths, cancers, radical cells, tumors, lesions, cysts, in every person, and also destroy all diabetes, high blood pressure, painful joints, backs, and knee ailments. Father, I ask you to give our homes, vehicles, businesses, restaurants, communities, finances, offices, properties, telephone lines, ministries, families, and friends total deliverance from unclean spirits and evil influences in the name of Jesus.

Heavenly Father, I ask you to fill each of us with your precious Holy Spirit and the fruit of the Spirit including Your love, joy, peace, Your goodness, meekness, faithfulness, Your patience, gentleness, and self-control. I pray that You will fill everyone I prayed for today with Your Holy Spirit anointing, and fill them with the peace, character, and nature of our Lord and Savior Jesus Christ. I ask You Lord Jesus to wash and cleanse their minds with Your precious blood, and give them clarity of though. I command that our minds, will, and emotions be submitted to Christ. To God be the Glory. Amen!

SUNDAY - DAY 1

Pray for your family, pastors, ministers, church leaders, teachers, and church members.

MEDITATION PSALM – 3

1 Lord, how are they increased that trouble me! many are they that rise up against me.

2 Many there be which say of my soul, There is no help for him in God. Selah.

3 But thou, O Lord, art a shield for me; my glory, and the lifter up of mine head.

4 I cried unto the Lord with my voice, and he heard me out of his holy hill. Selah.

5 I laid me down and slept; I awaked; for the Lord sustained me.

6 I will not be afraid of ten thousands of people, that have set themselves against me round about.

7 Arise, O Lord; save me, O my God: for thou hast smitten all mine enemies upon the cheek bone; thou hast broken the teeth of the ungodly.

8 Salvation belongeth unto the Lord: thy blessing is upon thy people. Selah. [KJV]

A Seven Day Intercessory Prayer Journal

NAMES: _____

MONDAY – DAY 2

Intercede for our government(s), the president, appointed and elected officials-local, state, and national, implementation of fair laws and policies.

MEDITATION PSALM – 7:1-9

1 O Lord, rebuke me not in thine anger, neither chasten me in thy hot displeasure.

2 Have mercy upon me, O Lord; for I am weak: O Lord, heal me; for my bones are vexed.

3 My soul is also sore vexed: but thou, O Lord, how long?

4 Return, O Lord, deliver my soul: oh save me for thy mercies' sake.

5 For in death there is no remembrance of thee: in the grave who shall give thee thanks?

6 I am weary with my groaning; all the night make I my bed to swim; I water my couch with my tears.

7 Mine eye is consumed because of grief; it waxeth old because of all mine enemies.

8 Depart from me, all ye workers of iniquity; for the Lord hath heard the voice of my weeping.

9 The Lord hath heard my supplication; the Lord will receive my prayer…

A Seven Day Intercessory Prayer Journal

NAMES: _____

TUESDAY – DAY

Pray for unsaved souls in America and other nations, hospitals, mental and physical illness and diseases.

MEDITATION PSALM – 103:1-12

1 Bless the Lord, O my soul: and all that is within me, bless his holy name.

2 Bless the Lord, O my soul, and forget not all his benefits:

3 Who forgiveth all thine iniquities; who healeth all thy diseases;

4 Who redeemeth thy life from destruction; who crowneth thee with lovingkindness and tender mercies;

5 Who satisfieth thy mouth with good things; so that thy youth is renewed like the eagle's.

6 The Lord executeth righteousness and judgment for all that are oppressed.

7 He made known his ways unto Moses, his acts unto the children of Israel

8 The Lord is merciful and gracious, slow to anger, and plenteous in mercy.

9 He will not always chide: neither will he keep his anger for ever.

A Seven Day Intercessory Prayer Journal

NAMES: _____

10 He hath not dealt with us after our sins; nor rewarded us according to our iniquities.

11 For as the heaven is high above the earth, so great is his mercy toward them that fear him.

12 As far as the east is from the west....

A Seven Day Intercessory Prayer Journal

WEDNESDAY – DAY 4

Pray for our youth, physical and sexual abuses, drugs/alcohol, porno addictions, crime, inmates.

MEDITATION PSALM – 4

1 Hear me when I call, O God of my righteousness: thou hast enlarged me when I was in distress; have mercy upon me, and hear my prayer.

2 O ye sons of men, how long will ye turn my glory into shame? How long will ye love vanity, and seek after leasing? Selah.

3 But know that the Lord hath set apart him that is godly for himself: the Lord will hear when I call unto him.

4 Stand in awe, and sin not: commune with your own heart upon your bed, and be still. Selah.

5 Offer the sacrifices of righteousness, and put your trust in the Lord. 6 There be many that say, Who will show us any good? Lord, lift thou up the light of thy countenance upon us.

7 Thou hast put gladness in my heart, more than in the time that their corn and their wine increased.

8 I will both lay me down in peace, and sleep: for thou, Lord, only makest me dwell in safety.

A Seven Day Intercessory Prayer Journal

NAMES: _____

THURSDAY – DAY 5

Intercede for deliverance from demonic attacks: heavy burdens, bondage, debt, depression oppression, controlling spirits, and confusion.

MEDITATION PSALM- 140: 1-8

1 Deliver me, O Lord, from the evil man: preserve me from the violent man;

2 Which imagine mischiefs in their heart; continually are they gathered together for war.

3 They have sharpened their tongues like a serpent; adders' poison is under their lips. Selah.

4 Keep me, O Lord, from the hands of the wicked; preserve me from the violent man; who have purposed to overthrow my goings.

5 The proud have hid a snare for me, and cords; they have spread a net by the wayside; they have set gins for me. Selah.

6 I said unto the Lord, Thou art my God: hear the voice of my supplications, O Lord.

7 O God the Lord, the strength of my salvation, thou hast covered my head in the day of battle.

8 Grant not, O Lord, the desires of the wicked: further not his wicked device; lest they exalt themselves. Selah....

A Seven Day Intercessory Prayer Journal

NAMES: _____

FRIDAY -DAY 6

Intercede for marriages, relationships, friendships, family unity, lost loved ones, extended families, also bind untimely separation and divorce.

MEDITATION PSALM: 147:1-10

1 Praise ye the Lord: for it is good to sing praises unto our God; for it is pleasant; and praise is comely.

2 The Lord doth build up Jerusalem: he gathereth together the outcasts of Israel.

3 He healeth the broken in heart, and bindeth up their wounds.

4 He telleth the number of the stars; he calleth them all by their names.

5 Great is our Lord, and of great power: his understanding is infinite.

6 The Lord lifteth up the meek: he casteth the wicked down to the ground.

7 Sing unto the Lord with thanksgiving; sing praise upon the harp unto our God:

8 Who covereth the heaven with clouds, who prepareth rain for the earth, who maketh grass to grow upon the mountains.

9 He giveth to the beast his food, and to the young ravens which cry.

10 He delighteth not in the strength of the horse: he taketh not pleasure in the legs of a man....

A Seven Day Intercessory Prayer Journal

NAMES:

SATURDAY -DAY 7

Intercede for spiritual anointing, empowerment, goals, God's plan and purpose, direction, destiny, creativity, wholeness-mind, body, and soul.

MEDATION PSALM 25:1-9

1 Unto thee, O Lord, do I lift up my soul.

2 O my God, I trust in thee: let me not be ashamed, let not mine enemies triumph over me.

3 Yea, let none that wait on thee be ashamed: let them be ashamed which transgress without cause.

4 Shew me thy ways, O Lord; teach me thy paths.

5 Lead me in thy truth, and teach me: for thou art the God of my salvation; on thee do I wait all the day.

6 Remember, O Lord, thy tender mercies and thy loving kindnesses; for they have been ever of old.

7 Remember not the sins of my youth, nor my transgressions: according to thy mercy remember thou me for thy goodness' sake, O Lord.

8 Good and upright is the Lord: therefore will he teach sinners in the way.

9 The meek will he guide in judgment: and the meek will he teach his way....

A Seven Day Intercessory Prayer Journal

NAMES: _____

References

Damazio, Frank. *Seasons of Intercession: God's Call to Prayer Intercession for Every Believer.* Portland, Oregon: City Bible Publishing, 1998.

Hillebrenner, Bill. *"The Plainer Truth About Grace."* Indianapolis, IN: Barnabas Ministries, 2009.

Robertson, Norman. *Ministering in the Power of the Holy Spirit.* Matthews, NC: NRM Publications, 1994.

Robertson, Norman. *Walking in Victory.* Matthews, NC: NRM Publications, 1996.

Straughan, Walt. *God Wants You Healed.* Staunton, VA: Walt. Straughan Ministries, 1999.

Treat, Casey. *Renewing the Mind: The Foundations of Your Success.* Tulsa, Oklahoma: Harrison House Incorporated, 1999.

Winston, Bill. *The Kingdom of God in You: Discover the Greatness Of God's Power Within.* Tulsa, Oklahoma: Harrison House Incorporated, 2006.

Bible References

Unless otherwise indicated, all Scripture quotations are taken from the King James Version of the Bible.

Scripture quotations marked (AMP) are from the Amplified Bible. Zondervan Corporation, Grand Rapids, Michigan. 1987.

Scripture quotations marked (KJV) are from The King James Bible Version. Thomas Nelson Publishers, Nashville, Tennessee. 1997.

Scripture quotations marked (NKJV) are from the New King James Version. Thomas Nelson Publishers, Nashville, Tennesee. 1982.

Scripture quotations marked (NIV) are from the New International Version. Zondervan Corporation, Grand Rapids, Michigan. 2011.

Scripture quotations marked (NLT) are from the New Living Translation. Tyndale House Foundation. Carol Stream, Illinois. 2007.